WEST TEXAS Stories

I0801901

# West Texas Stories

Edited by

Glenn Dromgoole

Abilene Christian University Press

**WEST TEXAS STORIES**

ACU PRESS

Copyright © 2016 by Glenn Dromgoole

ISBN 978-0-89112-469-674-4
LCCN 2016025232

Printed in the United States of America

ALL RIGHTS RESERVED
No part of this publication may be reproduced, stored in a retrieval system, or transmitted in any form by any means—electronic, mechanical, photocopying, recording, or otherwise—without prior written consent.

LIBRARY OF CONGRESS CATALOGING-IN-PUBLICATION DATA
Names: Dromgoole, Glenn, editor.
Title: West Texas stories / edited by Glenn Dromgoole.
Description: Abilene, Texas : Abilene Christian University Press, [2016]
Identifiers: LCCN 2016025232 (print) | LCCN 2016026112 (ebook) | ISBN 9780891124900 (trade paper) | ISBN 9780891126744 (e-book)
Subjects: LCSH: Texas, West—History—Anecdotes. | Texas, West—Biography—Anecdotes. | Texas, West—Social life and customs—Anecdotes. | LCGFT: Anecdotes.
Classification: LCC F386.6 .W47 2016 (print) | LCC F386.6 (ebook) | DDC 976.4/9—dc23
LC record available at https://lccn.loc.gov/2016025232

Cover design by Greg Golden
Interior text design by Sandy Armstrong

For information contact:
Abilene Christian University Press
ACU Box 29138
Abilene, Texas 79699

1-877-816-4455
www.acupressbooks.com

16 17 18 19 20 21 22 / 7 6 5 4 3 2 1

# Contents

# Introduction

"When it comes to good stories," the late, great San Angelo novelist Elmer Kelton admitted, "I am as shameless a thief as you'll meet." You can read what he means by that in the concluding piece in this collection—one of my favorites—"Fiction Writers Are Liars and Thieves."

Well, I didn't *steal* the more than three dozen stories included in *West Texas Stories*, but I did enjoy borrowing them and perhaps giving them some new life. Mostly, I enjoyed reading them, some for the first time, others that have been personal favorites for years. I hope you will like reading them as well.

What I looked for in putting together this collection were stories that stand the test of time, that offer a glimpse into the history and culture of this huge part of the state that we call West Texas, and that can be told in a few pages. Some of the tales are amusing, some are nostalgic, some historical, some dramatic, some personal.

I present them here in pretty much chronological order, beginning with several stories from the West Texas frontier, continuing through the first half of the twentieth century, and on to more modern days.

Quite a few of the pieces were excerpted from books, and I appreciate the publishers and authors who gave permission to reprint them here. I hope these passages might encourage some readers to want to plunge more deeply into the subject matter and read the complete original texts.

A special thanks to my friends at Abilene Christian University Press for their encouragement and support in this project. The idea for *West Texas Stories* grew out of a previous collection of *West Texas Christmas Stories* that I compiled and edited a few years ago. Consider this a companion anthology, a first cousin perhaps.

I have a personal fondness for collections like this, probably because they are well suited to my own short attention span. Maybe yours as well.

Happy reading.

*Glenn Dromgoole*

*Publisher's Note: Three of our stories allude to "Indians," a historically used, blanket term for Native Americans on the Western Frontier. Unfortunately, many of the details of the peoples and cultures referenced here remain unknown.*

*Interwoven: A Pioneer Chronicle* by Sallie Reynolds Matthews covers the period 1861 to 1899 and focuses on the Reynolds and Matthews ranching families of Albany. It is considered one of the top Texas books about early-day ranching, especially from a woman's point of view. In this unedited story, Matthews tells about the time her brother, George Reynolds, was shot in the stomach by an arrow.

# An Arrow in the Stomach

Sallie Reynolds Matthews

In April 1867, some horses had been stolen from settlers east of us and a party of men, riding in hot haste to overtake the Indian marauders, came to our ranch where they were joined by my brothers, George and William, and Si Hough.

They overtook the Indians at the Double Mountain Fork of the Brazos, a distance of thirty-five or forty miles from the Stone Ranch. The Indians were loitering there, taking their ease and shooting buffaloes, thinking they were out of the danger zone. They were outnumbered, there being ten white men to seven Indians. One of our men, John Anderson, was shot through the arm, receiving a flesh wound, and a minie ball passed through William's sleeve.

Brother George was the only one seriously hurt. He was shot with an arrow that entered his body just above the navel. He was wearing a U.S. Army belt buckle about two inches wide by three long. This buckle may have saved his life, as the arrow hit the edge of the buckle, breaking the force of the shot to some extent or it would doubtless have gone through his body.

He pulled the shaft out, but the head was left in his body, where it stayed fifteen years. At first they thought it might have dropped in the loose sand when the shaft was taken out and had been covered, but that was not the case, as was proven in later years.

When Si came up and saw George lying there, he swore he would have the scalp of the Indian who shot him. He was not long getting it.

William and John Anderson rode all night to tell the family what had happened. The night before they came, my father had a dream which so impressed him that he told Mother that one of the boys was wounded, and he was walking the yard in distress and looking for a messenger when the two boys came. This premonition seemed almost psychic.

How to get the wounded boy home was a problem. They tied two horses together, heads and tails, and filled in between with their packs, called kayaks, made of cowhide and on the order of old-fashioned saddlebags. These were placed across the horses and filled in with bedding, and the wounded man was laid on this improvised bed. A man on each side led the horses as the slow journey home was begun.

You can realize that this mode of travel was almost unbearable, but he endured it until nearing home, when he asked to be put upon his horse, which had an easy gait. He wanted the family to see him sitting on his horse!

They, of course, did not know that he was still alive. When the scouting party approached the ranch, the younger boys were on top of the smokehouse watching, and when they counted the full number it was a great relief and joy to those at home.

In the meantime, Sam Newcomb was riding night and day to Weatherford, more than a hundred miles away, for a doctor, only stopping for a bite to eat and a fresh horse at the ranches along the way. He and Dr. James D. Ray of Weatherford rode day and night on the return trip. When the doctor arrived, he probed the wound a little and that ended his treatment. It was all he could do at that time as he did not have the facilities of modern surgery.

Strange to say, the wound healed without infection and soon George was going about as usual. However, he suffered a good deal of pain in his body until the arrow was removed, although no one would have suspected this from the active life he led.

The arrowhead either went into the muscles of the back at first, or in some manner gradually worked its way to the back. Years afterward there was a knot pushed out near his spine which he suspected was the arrowhead coming to the surface. He was right, and in 1882 he went to Kansas City and had it taken out.

No anesthetic was used, and before going into the operation he exacted a promise from the doctor that he would stop when asked. Two friends went into the operating room with him to see him through. One of them ran out as soon as the doctor started work. The other, "Shanghai" Pierce, a well-known cattleman of South Texas, became so excited when he saw the deep incision that he yelled, "Stop, doctor, you are cutting that man to the hollow."

At this, my brother called a halt. The cut had missed the arrowhead and had gone down by the side of it. Brother raised himself to a sitting posture and bent forward. The steel arrowhead slipped out into the incision.

Reprinted from *Interwoven: A Pioneer Chronicle* by Sally Reynolds Matthews, by permission of Texas A&M University Press, Copyright 1936 Sallie Reynolds Matthews, 1958, 1982 Watkins Reynolds Matthews.

Ross McSwain wrote a column called Out Yonder for the *San Angelo Standard-Times* about West Texas people, places, and stories. Some of the pieces, including this one, were later collected into a book, *Tales from Out Yonder.*

# Indian Emily: Fact or Fiction?

Ross McSwain

It's only proper that stories from the frontier be truthful, and my hat is off to the folks at Fort Davis in far West Texas for setting the record straight on Indian Emily, despite the fact that their action has ruined a wonderful love story.

As many travelers to Fort Davis know, Indian Emily was the young Apache girl who is supposed to have saved the post—Fort Davis—from surprise attack when she alerted her lover, a young army lieutenant, that the hostiles were coming. The state of Texas erected a historical marker to her memory in 1936, and the love story-adventure was written up by several people, including Fort Davis's distinguished historian Barry Scobee, who even reiterated the words that Emily is said to have uttered to a fort sentry just before she died.

Through the years, Indian Emily's story has been a central theme surrounding a number of activities held in the West Texas community. The story has helped attract many tourists to the fort and also indirectly helped draw attention to restoring the fort buildings and ruins during early years of preservation.

Unfortunately, the story is not true but merely a legend, say fort historians. Thus, Indian Emily's historic marker located in the old fort cemetery has been removed for storage in the fort's archives.

Since Indian Emily's story was first published in Carl Raht's wonderful book *The Romance of the Davis Mountains and the Big Bend Country* in 1919, the tale of the Indian girl's romance with the army officer has been published throughout the country and has been featured in films, television, books, magazines, and newspapers. The story goes something like this:

Emily, an Apache maiden, was wounded and captured by troopers out of Fort Davis in the late 1860s. She was taken to the fort, where she was nursed back to health by a Mrs. Eason. The Indian girl grew up on the post and eventually fell in love with Mrs. Eason's son, Lieutenant

Tom Eason. When the soldier married a girl of his own race, Indian Emily was heartbroken and returned to her Apache tribe.

Later, as the story goes, she overhears a plan for an Apache assault on the fort. In an act of selfless love, she slips away in the middle of the night to warn the young officer, Eason. As she approaches the fort, a nervous sentry shoots her when she fails to answer his challenge. She died in the arms of Mrs. Eason after telling of her everlasting love for her son and of the impending attack on the fort. She was buried in the post cemetery and the marker that was erected by the state was placed on what was identified as her gravestone.

According to Raht and Scobee, the story had been confirmed in 1917 by Henry Flipper, the first African-American to graduate from West Point. Flipper served for a time at Fort Davis and Fort Concho but left the army after being court-martialed for allegedly stealing money from the Fort Davis commissary. Flipper later went on to be a successful mining engineer and leading citizen of El Paso.

After lots of research, fort historians found that no Apache attack was ever planned or carried out. Also, the researchers found that there was never a Lieutenant Tom Eason assigned duty at the fort, and no person by that name ever served in the U.S. Army prior to 1903.

Historians have found additional flaws in the story as well, including the fact that Emily did not behave like an Apache woman, and that Apache women never took part in any attack or did any fighting except in dire circumstances.

One historian's theory is the story was generated by someone "reading Victorian romances," and it was passed along as a true event.

Even though historians are now sure that such an event never took place and that there was never an Indian Emily, some quietly admit that "we can't prove it didn't happen, either."

The late great Texas folklorist J. Frank Dobie used to have a saying about such stories. "Perhaps it didn't happen that way, but it should have." The story of Indian Emily is still an enchanting one like many others about events that have taken place in our state.

Reprinted by permission of Jean McSwain and the *San Angelo Standard-Times.*

Army Lieutenant Henry Kirby was assigned to the Tenth Infantry stationed at Fort McKavett in 1878. On his way from San Antonio to assume his post, however, he was the victim of a stagecoach robbery. In a letter, Kirby described the experience.

# Stagecoach Robbery

Henry Kirby

Having heard in San Antonio of two recent murders on my road, I purchased a large revolver before leaving. I set out alone in a tolerably comfortable coach. Twelve miles out, we met a conveyance containing the corpse of a young man who had been murdered the night before, a few steps from the road. This did not make me feel very comfortable nor tend to lessen my vigilance.

I reached Fredericksburg late at night, took a room at the hotel, and slept till five in the morning. Our coach was changed here for a vehicle resembling an ambulance but not so good, and having no hinged doors, just simple openings which could be closed only by curtains fastened on the outside by small staples and pins.

I again set out, this time in company with Mr. Blacker, a district judge in western Texas. At Mason, we were joined by a drummer (traveling salesman) from New Orleans.

Feeling now quite secure, I forgot all about danger and about 11 P.M. dropped into a doze from which I was awakened by a man yelling at the driver to turn out from the road or he would blow his head off.

The judge and I were on the back seat, the drummer on the front, and our packages and valises on the bottom. The curtain was fastened down on my side, and I could only see or get out on the judge's side. Looking through this opening I saw a man about ten yards off, pointing a gun directly at the door.

I seized my pistols, which I had unbuckled and laid on the seat, and offered one to the judge, asking him to use it. But he declined, saying, "There is no use; there is a large gang of them, and we will all be killed if we resist." I then offered it to the drummer, but he refused, being busy stowing away his money and, as he afterwards said, looking to see if he could jump out and run.

I aimed at the only man I could see, but the judge caught my pistol and begged me not to fire. I told him that I did not propose to be robbed without fighting, but he insisted that there was a large gang and that resistance would be rashness. As by this time the only man I could have shot had gotten out of view, I concluded that it would be better to surrender.

The stage was driven about two hundred yards from the road, and we were ordered to get out, one at a time, without arms. As I was the last, I had time to take all my money except five dollars and put it down my left bootleg, putting my small pistol down my right boot and my watch in the case of a pillow lying on the seat.

As soon as I was out, they took me to the rear of the coach and demanded my money. I gave them my purse, and they, finding but five dollars in it, swore that I had more money, and that if I did not tell them where it was they would blow my brains out in case they found it. They then searched me, taking the studs from my shirt and, not finding any money, repeated their threats. I told them they might search as thoroughly as they pleased and suggested that they had better look in my boots, but as I expected they declined with an oath.

I was sent then to join the other passengers at the head of the team, and they proceeded to search the coach, which they did so thoroughly that they found some money that the judge had hidden in the straw, and also my watch. They cut our valises all to pieces, completely ruining them. They then searched me a second time, tearing the lining from my hat, and were about to let me go, when one of them said, "Make the scoundrel pull off his boots anyway."

Now if you have never looked down the barrel of a six-shooter within a few feet of your head, I can assure you that it is not pleasant, especially when it is held by a man whom you have no reason to doubt will pull the trigger under certain conditions, which conditions are pretty certain to be fulfilled in the next minute or two. I made a desperate resolve that, should they find the money, I would close in with the nearest robber and sell my life as dearly as possible.

I pulled off my right boot first, telling them that I had a pistol in it. While they are searching this and looking at the pistol, I pulled the other boot off cautiously, pressing my heel against the roll of money, and succeeded in throwing it out on the ground, and when they looked in the boot, it was empty. They then gave me back the small pistol.

We were told to get back in the coach and not make a sound or strike a light. Then the robbers rode off. We obeyed, to the letter, the order concerning noise and lights, but during the time I got out, crawled around on the ground, and found my money.

Adapted from a letter published in the 1949 *West Texas Historical Association Yearbook.*

J. Wright Mooar was one of the best-known buffalo hunters of the American frontier. Late in his life, he told stories about his buffalo-hunting years to James Winford Hunt, the founding president of McMurry University. They were published as a series in *Holland's* magazine in 1933, and in 2005 they were collected into a book, *Buffalo Days: Stories from J. Wright Mooar.* This is one of those stories

# The Frozen Robe

J. Wright Mooar as told to James Winford Hunt

It was the winter of 1879. Jim Ennis and his buffalo-hunting outfit were camped on a creek in Scurry County, Texas. The creek was later named for him—Ennis Creek. The buffalo had seemingly drifted from the breaks in the immediate vicinity of the camp; and one clear bright October morning, Jim told the boys he was going to do a little scouting. If they heard him shooting, they were to locate him and bring a wagon and some skinners to secure the hides and hams of the game he had killed.

The morning was what old-timers called a "weather breeder," calm and cold and clear. You could hear a twig snap for a hundred yards. A gunshot would carry for two or three miles. The dun prairie grass was coated with a heavy frost, and all nature seemed waiting and expecting something.

Jim rode from butte to butte and threaded the little draws and finally galloped out onto rolling prairies, where the scrubby mesquite was a miniature forest on the undulating terrain.

Noon came, and he had drifted some ten or twelve miles from camp without seeing a buffalo. Wandering herds of antelope gazed curiously at the hunter and then turned and fled like shadows, the gleam of sun on red backs and white sides marking their fleet retreat through the brush in kaleidoscopic patterns. Frequently a coyote skulking through the brush would glance inquiringly at the invader and then run with long leaping bounds to safer distance.

He found a small herd about two o'clock, quickly slipped into gun range, and the slaughter began. A big one fell at the first shot, and for a few minutes the others circled about bellowing as they smelled the blood. He downed two or three more while this was going on and followed as the herd finally began to run. For several miles, alternately riding and stalking, he hung on the flank of the herd, and during the passing of an hour a string of fallen animals marked his deadly progress.

As last he found himself on foot about one hundred yards from his horse and confronted with a wounded bull, which had suddenly turned upon him as he was trying to get in a death shot.

With a hoarse bellow, the bull charged. Ennis fired hastily—too hastily. The bull came swiftly on. Ennis dropped his gun and dashed to the largest mesquite, some twelve or fifteen feet high, and scrambled desperately into its branches, the thorns tearing his flesh and clothing. The bull crashed head-on against the gnarled trunk, which gave way, and Ennis was hurled to the ground.

He would have been killed by the infuriated animal, but a strange thing occurred, which at any other time would have been ludicrous in the extreme. A large dry branch broke from the tree and fell in a perfect fork over the bull's neck, the twigs and brush rattling about his head.

With a bellow of terror, the animal plunged aside and tore madly across the prairie, the branch clinging like a leech. His tail was alternately wildly waving like a signal of distress or standing rigidly out in an eloquent gesture of utter consternation, as bucking and bawling he disappeared down a coulee; and Ennis saw him no more.

With a sign of thankfulness for his escape, the hunter secured his rifle and looked about for his horse. It was then that he became aware of a sudden change in the weather.

The sky was heavily overcast with clouds, and dense fog banks soon shut off even the nearby landscape. His horse was not in sight. He paused to listen intently, hoping to hear the horse stamp or move about.

A peculiar sighing moan seemed to quiver all about him. Experience had taught him the meaning of such a phenomenon. Suddenly a herd of antelope scurried by, and then the first rush of the approaching norther, icy cold, rattled the branches of the mesquites and tugged at him as he braced against it. He whistled and called to his horse, but there was no response.

Desperate as his situation appeared, he was not at first alarmed. Using all his plains craft, he began to strive to locate himself. He reasoned that he was northeast of the camp and started to drift diagonally with the rising wind, which he felt sure was blowing from practically due north.

For some time, he wandered on, and dropped down into a little draw. He had about decided to hunt the shelter of a bluff or cave and hole up for the night, when he blundered upon the body of a buffalo he had shot earlier in the afternoon. Darkness, ending the short winter day, was now coming on, and the cold was piercing. Drawing his big hunting knife, he began to rip the skin from the carcass. With the skill of long practice, he soon had the great hide off. He cut some slices of meat from a hind quarter of the buffalo.

In the lee of the carcass a fire was soon glowing and the sliced meat quickly roasted. Darkness, howling wind, and spitting snow now made it imperative that shelter be found, but his plan was already perfected. Instead of wandering in cold and darkness seeking shelter, he decided to roll himself in the buffalo skin, hair side in, and lie down in the lee of the big body of the animal. Here, with his rifle beside him, he quickly ensconced himself, thanking his lucky stars for hot food and such shelter.

The heavy robe completely cut out the wind and he soon fell asleep. Some hours passed. The storm began to abate and the clouds broke and drifted away. A thick skiff of snow lay over the world, and the big stars looked down on the weirdly wild scene.

A long howl quivered through the night. It was quickly answered by a wild ululation from all directions. A big wolf—a fierce lobo of the Texas frontier—slipped out of the brush and fixed his avid eyes on the carcass, his mouth slavering. For a moment he sat on his haunches, and a soft whine followed by a deep snarl trembled in his throat. Flattening on the ground, he waited while his predatory companions gathered noiselessly about him. Then he rushed. In a moment the snarling pack was tearing at the frozen carcass.

In the midst of the savage feast, Ennis awoke. For a few moments he listened, his hand on his gun. Then he became aware that the wolves were also tearing at the skin in which he was rolled, and they began to trample him and drag and roll him about. He decided it was time to break up the festivities, if he was not to be eaten alive. But when he essayed to roll out of the skin he found he was solidly encased.

It had frozen!

The wolves were all over him snarling and tearing at the hide, and his imagination began to picture his slow doom, dying in agony, literally eaten alive.

Horror fell upon him and he struggled fiercely to extricate himself. As he tumbled and flopped about, his movements excited the wolves to fiercer activity. Realizing this, he lay perfectly still, using all his iron will to stay his throbbing nerves and twitching muscles.

The wolves now worried over him for what seemed ages. The cold sweat of fear streamed over his body. Life at times seemed passing from him. He was helpless and being eaten alive. He fancied he could feel the sharp agony of tearing teeth. Ages seemed to drag out their interminable intervals. Still the wolves fought over him.

Toughened frontiersman that he was, merciful unconsciousness came to him. When he returned to a realization of his surroundings, the pack was gone. He was alive and unhurt. He struggled and the robe loosened and fell apart. He rolled out. The sun was shining and deep stillness reigned in the wake of the brief norther.

Staggering from the folds of living death, dazed and trembling, he sought his horse. The animal was gone.

For hours he walked, seeking the camp, and at last came into it, staggering as he marched. His companions had just rounded up his horse, which had wandered in, and had become alarmed for his safety. As he approached, he was not recognized, but his gun was.

A man came toward him, drew a pistol, and demanded, "Old man, where did you get that gun?"

Though still dazed, he replied: "Same one I left camp with yesterday."

The hunters gathered about him in amazement as recognition of this stranger dawned. It was Jim Ennis, their leader.

He had left camp young, stalwart, raven-haired. He had returned, twenty-four hours later, aged, broken, and his hair as white as snow. From that terrible experience, he never recovered.

From *Buffalo Days: Stories from J. Wright Mooar* by J. Wright Mooar as told to James Winford Hunt, reprinted by permission of State House Press.

*Lester Galbreath of Albany, former park superintendent at Fort Griffin State Historic Site, is the author of Campfire Tales: True Stories from the Western Frontier. This unedited story is from his book.*

# One Long Night

Lester Galbreath

On a warm afternoon in the 1870s, several cowboys were driving a herd of cattle west of Fort Griffin. Two of the men, Jeff Turner and Smokey, rode ahead in search of water. Like many other men on the Texas frontier, "Smokey" was his nickname, his real name having been discarded for reasons unknown.

As they topped a rise, their attention was drawn to movement in the distance. Shading his eyes, Jeff could make out a patch of white. He soon discerned that it was a covered wagon; settlers or traders were venturing out onto the Staked Plains.

As the two men sat watching from their high vantage point, fifteen Indians came into view, traveling in a line that would intersect the wagon's path. The Indians had not as yet discovered the wagon, but if they kept riding in the same direction, they soon would. Smokey and Jeff knew they had to act quickly if the people in the wagon were to live out that afternoon.

Taking a route that would keep them out of the Indians' line of sight, they loped toward the settlers, trying to move noiselessly. They reached the wagon at dusk, and the family—a man, his wife, and their small son—had stopped for the night and was settling in to cook supper. Jeff told them about the Indians and pressed them to load the wagon immediately and depart. By the time everything was back in the wagon, it was nearly dark.

Abruptly, a shot rang out, and they knew the Indians had found them. Jeff yelled to the man to whip up the mules and make a run for it, while he and Smokey would stay back and try to detain the Indians as long as they could. The two cowboys jumped off their horses and knelt by the only cover available, a few scanty scrub bushes.

Complete darkness swallowed the scene as they pulled their guns, ready to take on the charging Indians. But tense silence prevailed. Each held his breath and strained his ears to hear the approaching Indians, but the lone sound was that of a wagon moving off into the distance.

They hunched frozen to the spot. They waited, and their imaginations showed them the Indians getting closer and closer. Their palms began to sweat, and the hair on the back of their necks stood up.

As they waited in the darkness, their minds told them to hold their ground and fight, but their feet demanded to run! Their feet won the argument, and they jumped up to flee. As they did, the Indians jumped up off the ground all around them, bullets and arrows flying. In the darkness and confusion, they broke through the enemy lines without a scratch, bursting out the other side at a dead run.

They weren't sure where they were or where they were going, but any place was better than where they'd been. Suddenly, the ground just dropped out from under them; they had run off the edge of a steep ravine. They fell, hit the rocky walls, rolled, fell again, slid hard, fell a few more feet, and finally landed with a thud. They managed to get to their feet and, after taking stock of their faculties, they found only scratches and bruises, no broken bones.

When they looked up, they could see at the top edges of the ravine some sky that was still lighted against the darker night sky. They saw that to the south the sky was lighter and to the north it was very dark. They knew then that the mouth of the canyon was to the south, so they started down the ravine in that direction. Soon they perceived moving shadows to the south and knew that the Indians had entered the canyon and were coming toward them.

Turning in that instant to the north, they walked until they came up against a solid rock wall. It was too dark to see, so they urgently felt along the rock with their hands, trying to find something to grip, to begin a climb out of the ravine. Finding nothing, Jeff told Smokey to stand on his shoulders so he could reach higher. As Jeff eased along the bluff allowing Smokey's hands to scrabble for any escape hold, Smokey suddenly said, "Wait! There's a little hole up here."

Jeff pushed while Smokey stretched and clawed along, finally managing to climb into a small opening that he hoped was a cave. The roof was very low, with only enough room for sitting. Smokey reached down and helped Jeff climb in. They wanted to get as far in as possible, for if the Indians found them in that little hole, they would be sitting ducks. The roof was too low for them to walk, but they could crawl on their hands and knees.

At first, they had believed this hole was just a small cave, so they were surprised that they could keep crawling in deeper and deeper. Eventually, they realized they could no longer feel the walls or the roof, so they slowly stood up. It was as their knees straightened that there came a loud buzzing. Everyone on the frontier dreaded that sound! They froze, afraid to move.

Jeff had two matches, and he struck one. In the flickering light, they could see that they were in a large room, and thousands of rattlesnakes were covering the floor—great balls of snakes unwinding and slithering in all directions. The match went out, and in the darkness they could hear—they could feel!—the snakes on all sides.

Hurriedly, Jeff lit the other match. The snakes were becoming more agitated, buzzing louder and louder. Then, that last match went out. Anyone who's ever been in a deep cave knows that the darkness in a cave is the blackest black ever seen. Jeff and Smokey strained every muscle in their bodies, trying not to move, not even to breathe, until finally they eased into a sitting position back to back, leaning against each other. With every animal instinct they wanted to run, but they did not know the way to the tunnel leading out.

After a while, Jeff started talking. He told Smokey that Indians had killed his wife and children several years before. He went on to say that if his time to die had come, he was ready. Suddenly, Jeff jerked, then told Smokey he had been bitten. Soon Jeff was thrashing about in great pain, talking wildly. Smokey tried to hold him, offering comfort while trying not to disturb the snakes. After a long time, Jeff became still, and Smokey knew that he had died.

Sitting in the darkness alone, Smokey endured through the terrifying night. After a long time, something strange appeared. It took a moment for Smokey's eyes to focus on the small beam of light in the distance. At first, he could not comprehend what he was seeing. Finally, he realized it must be morning, and sunlight was shining through the entry tunnel.

He had not heard the snakes for some time, and he did not know where they were. One thing was sure, though: He was leaving this tomb, no matter what. Crawling along and dragging Jeff's body, he reached the outside without encountering a snake. He lowered Jeff's body down on the face of the bluff to the ground, then jumped.

The morning sky revealed Indian tracks on the ground but no Indians in sight. Walking out of the ravine, he came upon the wagon and the family from the night before. They were cooking breakfast and told Smokey that a troop of cavalry returning to Fort Griffin had heard the attack and rushed to their rescue. The Indians, having decided that discretion was the better part of valor, had departed.

Smokey sat down to eat breakfast with the family, and to rest.

Before he had spent the night in the cave, Smokey had black hair, but when he left the cave, his hair was snow white.

Reprinted by permission of the author.

Tanner Laine was a longtime writer and regional editor with the *Lubbock Avalanche-Journal* who wrote stories about old-time cowboys and compiled them into a book, *Cow Country*, in 1969.

# Paul Revere of the Prairie

Tanner Laine

New England may have its famous ride of Paul Revere in days of the American Revolution, but just as thrilling was a fantastic 335-mile horseback dash made by a West Texas boy of ten back in the early days of the Old West, about the year 1881.

The lad was Bob Slaughter, son of Col. C. C. Slaughter, pioneer rancher. Young Bob grew up to be a leading cattleman in his own right. His heroic ride, from Dallas to German Springs just north of Big Spring, was a forty-one-hour nonstop adventure to save his father's huge Long S Ranch from a group of swindlers.

After the long ride across broken, unmarked prairie land, Bob got to the German Springs headquarters of the Long S too exhausted to speak. He made it in time to prevent usurpers from gaining possession of the ranch.

It seems that in 1881, at his offices in Dallas, Col. Slaughter had sold the Long S to an "English Lord" and associates for half a million dollars. He prepared transfers and a letter of introduction for giving possession to the new owners and dispatched them in a special stagecoach to the ranch, which covered parts of Howard, Borden, Martin, and Dawson counties.

Cagey rancher that he was, the Colonel had doubts. He cabled London for information on the group—and three days later learned they had misrepresented themselves. Their references and credit were false.

On a balmy summer night, Bob was dispatched on his famous ride. Clad only in shirtsleeves, weighing only a scant eighty pounds, the lad mounted a lightweight racing saddle about 9 P.M. and rode out of Dallas. He carried enough money to buy good replacement horses along the way. He also carried a letter of explanation.

The next morning young Slaughter had pounded into Weatherford and exchanged horses. He sped on through the Palo Pinto Mountains, out past Fort Phantom Hill, and stopped at the Sam Barnes Ranch at the mouth of Cottonwood Creek in the vicinity of present-day Abilene, where he again swapped horses.

At dawn the next day, a weary Bob spotted the English party camped at Rock Springs near the Colorado River in the Borden County area—not far from the Long S. He swung wide to avoid being seen by the fake nobility.

That afternoon he reached the ranch headquarters too worn out to speak. The ranch foreman found Col. Slaughter's note. The British party—which arrived the next day—was barred from the ranch.

The Englishmen returned to Dallas. Facing exposure, the imposters returned to England in a hurry!

It took young Bob several months to recover from his tortuous dash that drew the admiration of the rough-hewn early West. He later joined his father in operation of the Long S, which grazed up to fifty-five thousand head of cattle over a wide area of the Plains country.

Reprinted by permission of Tanner Laine's son, Tanner A. Laine.

Bill O'Neal of Carthage, author of more than forty books on Texas and western history, was named Texas State Historian in 2012.

# Old Tascosa: Gunfighter Capital of the Panhandle

Bill O'Neal

Tascosa, a rambunctious wolf howl of a town surrounded by big cattle ranches, became known as the "Cowboy Capital of the Panhandle." But during its 1880s heyday, Tascosa just as accurately could have been branded the "Gunfighter Capital of the Panhandle."

Tascosa came to life during the mid-1870s, when there was only one other town, Mobeetie, in the vast expanse of the Texas Panhandle. Enormous cattle ranches developed in the vicinity. The LS Ranch—the Lee Scott Cattle Company—grazed fifty thousand head of cattle on rangelands around Tascosa. Other enormous ranches in the region included Charles Goodnight's JA, The LIT, the Flying Pan, and the three-million-acre XIT.

During the 1880s, Tascosa's population reached four hundred. Assorted businesses dedicated to serving area ranches and cowboys were established along a two-block Main Street that ran east and west. An intersection was made by the Dodge City Trail, which ran south to north through the adobe town, then angled northeastward two hundred fifty miles to Dodge. A cluster of dives a quarter of a mile east of Main Street was dubbed "Hogtown," partially because of such less than glamorous sporting ladies as Homely Ann, Gizzard Lip, Rowdy Kate, Box Car Jane, Panhandle Nan, Slippery Sue, Canadian Lily, and Frog Lip Sadie.

In Tascosa's early years, the entire region was lawless. In 1878, Billy the Kid escaped the violence of New Mexico's Lincoln County War by driving a herd of stolen horses to Tascosa. The Kid was accompanied by four fellow gunmen/stock thieves: Tom O'Folliard, Henry Brown, Fred Waite, and John Middleton. Camping just south of town beside the Canadian River, the New Mexico gang engaged in horse racing and other forms of gambling. There were stories of a shooting match between the Kid and Temple Houston and Bat Masterson. But none of these noted shootists engaged in gunplay while in Tascosa. The Kid and O'Folliard soon went back to New

Mexico and their deaths. Middleton and Waite returned to their homes in Kansas and Oklahoma. Henry Brown stayed at Tascosa. He cowboyed for the LIT, took a job tracking horse thieves, and later pinned on a badge as deputy sheriff of newly organized Oldham County.

The initial resident of Boot Hill was Bob Russell, a former cowboy who operated a saloon in Tascosa, and who imbibed freely of his own liquid merchandise. In March 1881, Russell drunkenly stormed into the store of merchant Jules Howard, who saw him coming and stood with his six-gun already drawn. Russell fumbled for his revolver and triggered one wild shot, but he was drilled in the chest, head, and trigger finger. Russell was buried on a knoll west of town that began to be called Boot Hill.

The next August another gunshot victim was interred on Boot Hill. A trail herd was pastured near town, and foreman Fred Leigh led his crew into Tascosa for a drunken spree. Riding down the street, Leigh shot the head off a duck. Swaggering obnoxiously around the town, he clashed separately with Cape Willingham, first sheriff of Oldham County, and with Deputy Sheriff Henry Brown.

The two lawmen rounded up a four-man posse, then Sheriff Willingham confronted Leigh in front of the Equity Bar. When Leigh reached for his revolver, Willingham blasted him off his horse with a double-barreled shotgun.

Brown and the four possemen quickly closed in, and the surviving cowboys left town. Leigh's body was taken to Boot Hill.

In 1882, four fatal shootouts added to Tascosa's notorious reputation. In Hogtown, a gambler known as Mexican Frank Larque twisted his gun upward and fired through the bottom of the holster, fatally wounding Henry McCullar. Another fight erupted in Hogtown over a card game, and Louis Keyes was mortally wounded. Bill Yandell promptly palmed his revolver and shot Keyes's killer in the stomach.

In the fall of 1882, a drunken cowboy was shot in the head and robbed. Bartender Johnny Maley was widely suspected, so the victim's brother, Ed Norwood, stalked into Maley's bar and shot him to death. Norwood was locked up in the adobe county building, but his friends knocked a hole in the adobe wall and put the prisoner on a fast horse. (Within a couple of years a two-story stone courthouse and jail was erected, thus reducing the likelihood of escape.)

Tascosa's bloodiest shootout erupted at the town's main intersection at two o'clock in the morning of March 21, 1886. Four LS riders—Ed King, Fred Chilton, Frank Valley, and John Lang—left a dance in Hogtown after midnight to seek further recreation in Tascosa. Ed King dismounted at the intersection to join a girl named Sally

Emory. The Jenkins and Dunn Saloon, on the southeast corner of the intersection, was dark, but several customers stood on the porch and exchanged insults with Ed King.

Chilton, Valley, and King rode on toward the Equity Bar, when a gunshot from the porch dropped King in his tracks. Cowboy Len Woodruff, who had been trying to win Sally's affections, ran to the fallen King and fired a Winchester slug into his throat.

The other three LS cowboys pulled their revolvers and charged on foot into the rear of the darkened saloon. A barrage of gunfire exploded inside. Woodruff caught two bullets low in the abdomen, while his friend, Charley Emory, was hit in the leg. As Woodruff staggered away, Frank Valley gave chase, but was felled by a bullet in the left eye.

Jesse Sheets owned the North Star Restaurant next to the saloon. Normally he slept at his family home a couple of blocks to the south, but on this fateful night he decided to sleep in his restaurant. Awakened by the post-midnight gunfire, Sheets foolishly went to the saloon and appeared in the front doorway. Silhouetted in the bright moonlight, Sheets was killed by Fred Chilton with a bullet to the forehead.

But Chilton's gunflash brought two rounds tearing into his chest. Stunned, Chilton handed his six-gun to Lang and died. Lang retreated outside, furiously exchanging fire with the men in the saloon.

Two lawmen sprinted onto the scene, ending what became known as "The Big Fight." The Big Fight produced four dead and several wounded.

The three dead LS cowboys were laid out on the porch of Howard's General Store across the street. They were covered with a tarpaulin. The next morning four coffins were hammered together, and new black suits were placed on the deceased.

With Sheriff Jim East and several special deputies on duty, a long funeral cortège headed west of town toward Boot Hill. The three LS coffins were in a wagon, followed by buggies and pedestrians and mounted cowboys, riding by twos. Tascosa had no church or preacher, so the county judge presided. He read from an Episcopal prayer book, and ladies sang "Nearer My God to Thee." A service for Jesse Sheets was held immediately after the LS burials. The LS put up three identical tombstones for their men. (Souvenir hunters chipped away at these gravestones, but identical replacements have been set in place.)

The next year Boot Hill received another shooting victim. Pete Fulton was shot at point-blank range in a livery stable by John ("The Catfish Kid") Gough, a survivor of The Big Fight. Fulton, with his vest on fire, ran into the street shouting for help. But within moments he collapsed and died.

Tascosa's last fatal shootout erupted in 1889 in the Equity Bar with gunplay between gambler Tom Clark and Sheriff Jim East, who owned the saloon. A cottonwood beam in the middle of the room supported the roof and had been dressed with a hexagon-shaped column of planks. Sheriff East ducked behind the column for cover and shot Clark to death.

During Tascosa's 1880s heyday there were ten fatal gunfights in town. But rapid decline set in during the 1890s, and in 1915 the county seat was moved to Vega. The adobe buildings of Tascosa lost their roofs and crumbled into dirt piles.

Cal Farley's Boys Ranch now occupies the old town site. All that remains from the nineteenth century are the 1884 stone courthouse, the reconstructed frame school, and Boot Hill, last home of pioneer Tascosans who lived, fought, and died in the Cowboy/Gunfighter Capital of the Panhandle.

Published by permission of the author.

Dennis Roberson is the author of a wonderful book, *Winning 42: The Strategy and Lore of the National Game of Texas*, in which he notes, "There are two types of people in Texas: those who play 42 and those who need to learn." In the preface to his book, he tells how the game was invented in 1887.

# Baptists and 42

Dennis Roberson

If necessity is the mother of invention, then the great game of 42 was born of necessity. Thanks should also be given to human ingenuity and, let's say, a religious loophole.

The inauspicious beginning of 42 occurred in 1887 in the tiny Texas hamlet of Trappe Spring (now Garner), about forty-five miles west of Fort Worth. In those days, strong religious beliefs controlled the moral climate of such communities. Baptists were the law, and card playing was the devil's work. But if you want someone to do something, especially kids, tell them it's against the rules.

Two young Trappe Spring boys, twelve-year-old William Thomas and fourteen-year-old Walter Earl, really liked to play cards. They found the game of dominoes (legal in Baptist land), well, boring. The boys often hid up in the hayloft to play cards. One spring day, however, they were caught by one of their parents. The other three parents were summoned. The cards were burned and the boys got a whipping to boot.

Being the determined and inventive young men that they were, William and Walter set out to change things. But they didn't seek to rewrite the Baptists' bylaws; they simply exploited a loophole instead. If dominoes weren't sinful, why not play cards with dominoes? That's essentially what they did. For about four months, William and Walter devised and fine-tuned the rules for a card game with dominoes. And a darn good game it was: 42.

No more haylofts for William and Walter. No more whippings.

They introduced the game to their families. They taught it to their small community. And before you knew it, everyone was playing 42. William delivered fruit from his father's orchard to nearby Mineral Wells, and he taught those folks to play 42. Later the Thomases and Earls moved to Fannin County in northeast Texas, again introducing 42 to the locals.

The game began to spread across Texas like one of its great rivers. It was not only a fun game, but also good clean fellowship. When World War II hit, Texas military men took the game overseas and taught it to their countrymen.

The game is still most popular in Texas, where Halletsville hosts an annual state championship and the Texas Senior Games also crowns 42 champions each year. It is played in homes, churches, and clubs as well as impromptu neighborly get-togethers. Outside Texas, one has to search harder to find 42 players, but they're there. And they're passionate about the game.

Let's tip our hat to those good ol' Baptists for inspiring the birth of the great game of 42.

From *Winning 42: Strategy and Lore of the National Game of Texas* by Dennis Roberson, Copyright © 1997, 2000, 2004, 2009 by Dennis Roberson. Reprinted with the permission of The Permissions Company, Inc., on behalf of Texas Tech University Press (ttupress.org).

Hallie Crawford Stillwell's memoir, *I'll Gather My Geese*, recounts her experiences working with her husband on their ranch in the Big Bend area after they married in 1918. In this excerpt from the book, she tells about going to live at the ranch as a young bride.

# The Bride

Hallie Crawford Stillwell

It was July 29, 1918. I was a nervous bride-to-be and twenty years old. I should have been excited and elated that the handsomest and most eligible bachelor around had proposed marriage, but instead I could only think of Papa's words: "He's too old for you and he hasn't led a proper life. That man drinks and gambles too much. He's just not suitable for you, daughter!"

Still, I was a determined daughter even at that young age. I chose to marry Roy Stillwell against Mama's and Papa's words of advice. I had too much respect for my parents to blatantly defy them, so Roy and I just climbed into his Hudson Super-6, drove to the Brewster County Courthouse, got our marriage license, and imposed on my cousin, Sadie Crawford Harrington. After a quick ceremony at her house, we drove to Marathon and boarded the train for San Antonio, where we would spend our honeymoon at the Gunter Hotel.

Four days later we left San Antonio and headed home, where I was to present my new husband to Mama and Papa. I stumbled over my words very quickly. “Mama and Papa, Roy and I are married!” Roy and I stood side by side and waited.

After a few moments of tense silence, Papa rose and spoke. “Well, the die is cast! Y’all better sit down and have some supper.”

From that day forward, Roy was a member of my family. I had anticipated the worst and had gotten what I really hoped for, acceptance of Roy by my mother and father.

My father did question Roy extensively about our lives together. He asked Roy, “Are you going to be living in your house in Marathon?”

Roy was prompt to reply, “I own that house in Marathon, but the ranch is my home and Hallie will be living on the ranch with me. We will keep the house in town as a place to come when we need to be in town, which should not be very often.”

I knew Papa was not any too happy about my living that far from town, especially in a place so close to the Mexican border. Not only was Pancho Villa a renowned raider, but many Mexicans used his name as their scapegoat when they raided isolated ranches along the Rio Grande. Papa frowned, but only warned: "Just take good care of her."

Once we had visited with family and friends for a few days, Roy decided that we had better head for the ranch, a ride some seventy-five miles from Alpine and an all-day drive. As we rode along I could tell that Roy was somewhat apprehensive. He was polite and pointed out many interesting names and places along the way. I absorbed the beautiful surroundings and knew that I would be happy around the mountains and the cacti that protected the rough terrain. Once we were within ten miles of the ranch, Roy began to get quiet and looked quite concerned. I finally asked, "Roy, is something bothering you?"

"Well, Hallie, there has never been a woman living on my ranch. The cowhands and I have always taken care of everything and never felt we needed a woman. Now, these men are good men but they may need a while to get used to you."

As we drove up to the ranch house, I saw three rough-looking cowboys leaning against a brush arbor that was attached to a tiny shack that was the ranch headquarters. I really hadn't expected much but I was somewhat surprised by its size, one room about twelve feet by sixteen feet. Still, I kept my chin up.

Roy, being quite the gentleman, slid out of the car and came around to open my door. He allowed me to get out and then pointed toward the tiny house. "This is it!"

I started toward the house with Roy right behind me. "That woman schoolteacher won't last six months down here in this Godforsaken country," was the remark that I heard from one of the ranch hands as Roy and I made our way toward the arbor. I really did not pay too much attention to this remark because I knew it was one I was not supposed to hear. Roy either did not hear it or pretended not to hear it, and we walked up to the trio awaiting us.

The men showed respect by removing their hats and extending their hands, but I felt their discontent. They stood quietly under the arbor while Roy ushered me inside. It did not take long to survey the domain. The room contained a small wood cookstove with a smoke-blackened coffeepot, a huge black iron teakettle, and a few pots and pans. There was a small cabinet (usually referred to as a safe) and on it was a shelf where a water bucket and gourd dipper stood. Also in the room were one table, one chair, two wooden benches, and only one bedroll, a mass of rolled-up quilts wrapped in a tarp in the corner. I then realized that I would have to share that cowboy bedroll with Roy and that it would be our bed.

"Come on in, boys, let's fix a bite of supper," called Roy to the men waiting impatiently outside, as he immediately began to scrape ashes out of the stove.

I sat in a chair as those clumsy cowboys stomped into the house and began to cook our supper. Little did I know how efficient at camp cooking they were. The more they worked, the more in the way I felt. As those earlier words from the cowboys echoed through my mind, I became more determined to stay. I wanted desperately to make a go of my marriage regardless of the stinging remarks these men had made.

As I sat at the table to have my first meal in my new home, I again felt the coldness of the ranch hands' reception. They were ignoring me, and Roy was bending over backward to melt the icy atmosphere. I smiled at the hands' crude remarks and complimented the cooks. Not one of the three icebergs thawed that evening.

The only conversation consisted of shallow cutting remarks. "I reckon you'll be a goin' back to town most of the time," Lee said as he gathered the tin plates, three-pronged forks, and case knives to wash.

"No, I expect to live here with Roy, or I wouldn't have married him," I replied.

"It's no fittin' place fer a woman," mumbled Jona as he headed for the door.

"We have work ahead of us tomorrow, boys. See you in the morning," Roy said as he untied the bedroll, spread it on the floor, and prepared our bed for the night.

I watched as the three taciturn men picked up their bedrolls stacked under the arbor and retired to the barn. I was glad to have them out of my sight. They had been acting as if they owned Roy, I thought. I turned to say something to Roy and found him already in the bedroll. I fumbled around for a while, got myself ready for bed, and rolled in next to him.

"They will never own me," I muttered without thinking.

Roy, already half asleep, asked what I had said.

"Nothing, absolutely nothing," I whispered.

From *I'll Gather My Geese* by Hallie Crawford Stillwell, reprinted by permission of Texas A&M University Press, Copyright 1991 Hallie Crawford Stillwell.

As a child, James Bruce Frazier lived on the Cross Ell Ranch west of Big Spring from 1927 to 1935, but it would hold a place in his heart for all of his sixty-five years. He died in 1989. A collection of his stories, *What I Learned on the Ranch and Other Stories from a West Texas Childhood*, was published in 2003. "The Riding Calf" is from that book.

# The Riding Calf

James Bruce Frazier

One morning at milking time we found Brownie with a new calf. I didn't rush up to her but squatted down on my heels waiting for her to introduce us. Brownie, a proud mama, nudged the bull calf with her nose until he slowly stood up, first on swaying back legs, then on wobbly front feet.

As he swayed from side to side on four pink hooves, his mama washed his face and brushed the glistening coat into spit-curls using her long gray tongue. Brownie was a Jersey, but her baby was marked like his papa, with a Hereford white face and four white stockings. His coat was dark, almost black.

My breath came out in steam that frosty morning, and I felt that I should make the new baby a warm bed. In the corner where the wooden pen brought shelter from the north wind yet was open to the morning sun, I made a nest of sweet red-top cane and alfalfa. After his breakfast of his mama's first milk, he snuggled down for a morning nap, comfortable, clean, and cozy.

It was not long before he came to me in the mornings for a nibble of cottonseed cake or grains of maize eaten from my hand. As he grew I tried riding him, just as I did with all the milk-pen calves. Unlike the others that bucked and pitched, he would allow a certain amount of riding in the cow lot. He was gentle and friendly, this special black bull calf that met me every time I came to the corrals.

As days passed I rode him more and more inside the pens, until the time we went out in the water trap and then to the house and by the barn. At first, he went where he wanted to go until I taught him to turn by patting him on the neck and soon he would respond as well as a pony. If you have ridden both cows and horses, you know that horses are easier to sit upon, better padded. But a riding calf is such an oddity that it's worth the discomfort.

When the riding was done, he followed me around the ranch like a pet. We were friends. One day he climbed the front porch steps and just for fun—and because Mama was outside feeding her chickens—I opened the door and Riding Calf walked right into the living room and lay down on the hearth in front of the fireplace, making himself comfortable.

When Mama came in and caught us, he was curled up like a huge pussy cat taking a nap. She wanted to be angry but couldn't help laughing, and so she let him stay a little while. After that he came in several times and was always a gentleman, never once making a mess. Mama said, "You are just lucky he behaves because it will be up to you to clean up if he forgets his manners."

At night, Riding Calf stayed in the corrals with the other calves, but by day he was a special pet. As he grew our rides got longer until in the fall I rode him to the schoolhouse. During classes he waited patiently outside, and at recess the children took turns riding him. He shared their syrup biscuits and drank from the well bucket when the teachers were not watching.

Riding Calf was smart as a dog, quickly learning new tricks. He could shake hands, kneel to say his prayers, roll over and play dead, and with one end of a rope around his neck, take part in skip-rope. I could ride sitting on him backwards, steering with his tail in my hand. The girls laughed and squealed to see us do that one.

As he grew, I began to have ideas about becoming a rodeo clown. "THE BOY FROM THE CROSS ELL RANCH AND HIS RIDING CALF." I could see billboard signs pasted on barns and fences in my imagination. I could spend the summer going to rodeos earning cash money, Riding Calf and I performing between contests, riding in parades and the grand entry, me carrying a flag on a spear with the Cross Ell brand on it. Boys never run out of things to dream about.

One afternoon when I came home I didn't see Riding Calf. When I searched and could not find him, I was told, "We took your riding calf to the freezer locker plant today and he was slaughtered for winter meat, just like the others raised in the milk pen." My idea was grand, but it never worked out.

On a ranch everything has its place and purpose. Milk-pen calves always go to the freezer. I had not counted on it applying even to Riding Calf. I just thought he was too special. Life is like that. We each have a fate and no matter what we do along the way, we fulfill our purpose, even though we know some special tricks.

A half-Jersey bull would become a major problem on a ranch that produces purebred Hereford cattle, when you stop to think about it. He was fun while he was growing up, but I never took the trouble to train another calf. None of them seemed smart enough, and anyway I never had the time. Calves are born to be eaten.

Mr. Hartman, the Cross Ell foreman, said, "Son, you just trained the wrong animal. If you spent your time on a colt, by now you would have a good horse to ride."

"Never ride a calf, and never eat a horse." That is an important lesson I learned as I cried myself to sleep, lonesome for my friend, Riding Calf.

From *What I Learned on the Ranch and Other Stories from a West Texas Childhood* by James Bruce Frazier, reprinted by permission of Don Frazier and State House Press.

Leon Hale is best known as a Houston newspaper columnist, writing largely about East Texas for more than fifty years. But this piece, from his book *Texas Chronicles*, is set in the area west of Fort Worth known as the West Cross Timbers region where his grandparents lived.

# Brother Foster's Prayer

Leon Hale

Long ago, out in that West Cross Timbers country beyond Fort Worth, Brother Foster was famous for prayers that showed scope and style. I once heard him send up a Thanksgiving prayer that was major league in all respects, and he did it standing in the kitchen door on Grandma Hale's farm.

This old fellow was not really a preacher. But in rural regions at the time I am talking about, purebred and registered preachers were scarce and people made do with the nearest they had to the real article.

Brother Foster taught Sunday school, and did funerals, and went around comforting the sick and sorrowful, and generally made a satisfactory substitute for a pastor. My father used to say you could put a black hat on Brother Foster and hand him a Bible and a collection plate and he could pass for a preacher at a Baptist convention.

There were whispered stories that Brother Foster would even do you a quiet and slightly invalid wedding, in case of an emergency where the need for quick nuptials was beginning to show. But I don't know if that was true, and even if it was, then I figure the old gent was simply rendering a public service, so let it go.

His specialty was prayers on special occasions, like at Fourth of July picnics, ice cream suppers, Christmas gatherings, and other holiday affairs. It must have been in '31 or '32 that Brother Foster came to Grandma Hale's farm for Thanksgiving dinner. All the women, especially, counted it a social triumph to have Brother Foster for Thanksgiving. I don't know how we got him, as he was spread pretty thin over that region.

The meal was the occasion for the prayer, so it was delivered as the blessing. Or asking the blessing, as we said, or returning thanks.

When the formal invitation was issued—"Brother Foster, will you return thanks for us?"—that luminary backed away from the table and took up a position in the doorway that led to Grandma's kitchen. Evidently he felt a need to be isolated from the general bunch.

He was a big, heavy-shouldered fellow with deep-set eyes and wavy white hair and a mighty voice. My father used to say that they ruined a first-rate preacher when they put Brother Foster to following a mule across a cotton patch.

He waited for silence before he began. If silence took a full minute to arrive, still he waited. We were supposed to keep our heads bowed and our eyes closed but by that time I had perfected a system of looking around at things through eyes that seemed closed but really weren't.

Brother Foster stood with his legs slightly apart and his hands behind him and his chin elevated and his eyes closed. Just when you thought he would begin, a foot would scuff or a throat would clear and he would hold off a while longer. Even a calf, bawling for its mama out at the barn, would delay his beginning.

He started out quietly, and built volume as he went along. He began with the food and the blessed hands that prepared it. He called Grandma by name, and I learned later that this was a high blessing, to get your name sent up in a prayer by Brother Foster, and on Thanksgiving Day, at that.

From the women, he went to the men who tilled the land and brought forth its fruits. He went on to thank the Lord for the beasts that pulled the plows, and those that sacrificed their lives to give us sustenance.

Then he took up the children and asked the Lord to bless their little hearts and keep them safe. (It didn't occur to me that he seemed to rank children behind mules and poultry, since this was before the age of child worship.)

He went into the field of medicine and thanked the Lord for protecting those of us who hadn't caught terrible diseases or suffered crippling injuries. He got into agriculture and mentioned the good corn crop, and the cotton crop which was fair. Went then to meteorology and pointed out to God that the rains came a little too late in the season but were appreciated anyhow.

He called the names of people who had died during the year, people we knew, and he gave thanks for their lives. He gave thanks for breezes that turned windmills, for pretty music, for the love of friends and kinfolks, for the very roof over our heads, for feather mattresses on cold winter nights.

This litany went on until the dressing was cold, and I thought it was more a sermon than a prayer. Not until a good many years later did I understand why Brother Foster's long prayers were sought and appreciated.

Life in that country was hard, and those folks needed somebody to remind them that they had a lot to be thankful for.

From *Texas Chronicles* by Leon Hale, reprinted by permission of the author.

Texas historian, storyteller, and museum director T. Lindsay Baker included this story in his collection of *More Texas Stories I Like to Tell My Friends*, published in 2012.

# Mrs. Jasper's Butter

T. Lindsay Baker

Mrs. Jasper at Claude, Texas, churned butter during the days of the Great Depression when no one ever wasted anything.

One day, the story goes, as Mrs. Jasper was churning, a little mouse ran across the top of the churn and fell into the milk. Mrs. Jasper reached in and got him out right quick, and since she didn't want to waste the milk she kept on churning and made herself a pound of butter out of the milk that the mouse had fallen in.

In the 1930s, everybody came in from the farms on Saturday and sold their butter and eggs at the store. Mrs. Jasper went into the store in Claude operated by Mr. Collins, and told her story.

"Mr. Collins, while I was churning this butter," she said, "a little mouse ran across the top of the churn and fell into the milk. I got him right out, and I don't think he hurt anything." Then she continued, "Since I know he was in there, I'd rather not eat that butter myself. But would you be willing to take this pound of butter and trade it for one that someone else has brought in? If they don't know that the mouse has been in there, it won't hurt anything."

The grocer thought about the proposition and wondered how he could deal with the situation. He didn't want to lose Mrs. Jasper's trade. Finally, he told her that he would be willing to make the trade since she was a regular customer. He asked her to come back for the fresh butter when she had finished her other shopping.

Mrs. Jasper went on about her errands in town, buying what small items that she needed for the coming week. In the meantime, grocer Collins proceeded with his work at the store between sales to customers. He took Mrs. Jasper's pound of butter into the back of the store. There he remolded the butter in his own mold and wrapped it neatly in paper the same way that he did all the other butter that farmers and their wives brought into town for him to sell to the townspeople. No one could tell the pound of Mrs. Jasper's butter from any others.

After making her rounds, Mrs. Jasper came back to the store to pick up the butter Mr. Collins had prepared for her in the supposed trade. Only he knew that the pound of butter he handed across the counter to Mrs. Jasper was the same one that she had brought in earlier.

Grocer Collins had come to the same conclusion that Mrs. Jasper had earlier: "If the buyer doesn't know anything about it, well then it won't hurt anything."

From *More Texas Stories I Like to Tell My Friends* by T. Lindsay Baker, reprinted by permission of Abilene Christian University Press.

Bob Green of Albany was a rancher, civic leader, historian, and a great storyteller. He died in 2009.

# Mary Anna's Ride

Bob Green

My parents married later in life than do most people but since both wanted a family, they tried to make up for their late start by having four children in seven years. I was the youngest of the four, born when my mother was forty-one and my father fifty-eight years old.

I still marvel at the way they endured the rearing of four active young children at their late age, when most people of their longevity were content just to enjoy the occasional company of their grandchildren. Mercifully, my older parents were spared the knowledge of some of the worst of the shenanigans concocted by their offspring.

One of the more memorable incidents they were innocently involved in happened back in the 1930s, when

I was twelve and my sister, Mary Anna, was fourteen. Bill and Tom, our two older brothers, were attending a military school in Roswell, New Mexico. Parents Day was coming up and my parents had promised "the boys" that they would be there.

An unusually long period of wet weather across West Texas and eastern New Mexico had made them uneasy about the condition of the roads they had to travel to get there. Now this was before much of the exploration and drilling of oil wells in that region that brought many modern improvements to the thinly settled countryside of West Texas and southeastern New Mexico, such as paved roads.

In the 1930s, the shortest route to Roswell from Albany was the same as it is today: Albany-Post-Tahoka-Brownfield-Plains-Tatum-Roswell, but there was one big difference. When you drove west out of Brownfield, Texas, you left the last paved road you would see until you reached Roswell, one hundred and fifty miles away.

Ordinarily, unpaved roads wouldn't have been much of an obstacle to my parents. They were both raised in the country and were accustomed to poor roads. But now they were faced with the situation of a rare, prolonged period of wet weather and they were fully aware that portions of the unpaved road between Brownfield and Roswell might become treacherous, if not downright impassable. With Parents Day drawing near, a decision had to be made soon about actually going.

My dad had a good friend who ranched between Plains, Texas, and Tatum, New Mexico, so he called him up and asked about the road conditions. The news was not encouraging. All the roads between Plains and Tatum were impassable. My dad reported what he had learned from his friend and said it appeared they probably would have to skip Parents Day.

Mother, her blue eyes flashing dangerously, replied in a firm, steady voice that "the boys" had been expecting us for days and were not going to be disappointed. We had a new car and could just leave a day early and go by way of Midland, Pecos, and Carlsbad to Roswell. According to the road map she clutched in her hand and had been studying, that route had paved roads all the way.

It's a long way from Albany to Roswell any way you go, but by the route we took back then it was really a long way. "The Great Circle Route," my father called it, as we left our ranch home early in the morning and headed west down old Highway 80. Old Highway 80 was sure not any four-lane divided roadway like its replacement, Interstate 20, is today, but it was paved.

Mother had contacted old friends who lived between Midland and Odessa and they insisted that we spend the night with them, so after a long, tedious drive, we arrived at the ranch home of Mr. and Mrs. Roy Parks. After supper the adults had a lot of catching up to do, so although Mary Anna and I were put to bed at a decent hour, the older ones sat up very, very late reminiscing.

The next morning, true to their ranching upbringing, everyone was up at dawn. After a tiresome drive, we finally reached Pecos in time for a late lunch at a restaurant the Parkses had highly recommended. Dad, always a heavy eater, really loaded up at the table. It became a somewhat extended lunch period, and Mother became nervous that we were falling so far behind her schedule to get us to Roswell on time. Finally, she insisted that we quit eating and get going, so we did.

In those days, highways weren't marked with anything like as many signs as they are today, so Dad got instructions at the café to get on the right one to Carlsbad. When we found it, we were pleased to discover that it was a brand new concrete highway, so we continued our journey on the smooth, straight road.

This was long before cars had air conditioning, and even with all the windows rolled down, the car soon became very warm as the afternoon progressed. The new highway we were traveling seemed to be completely deserted except for us. Before long, a troubling development arose as Dad's head began to nod, then sag, then droop as the car began to weave and meander all over the highway. The late hours of the previous evening combined with the huge meal he had just consumed and the hot temperature in the car had made Dad mighty drowsy.

After shaking himself several times, he finally gave up trying to keep his eyes open and pulled off onto the shoulder of the road and stopped. Turning the engine off, he leaned his head to one side against the door frame, closed his eyes, and seemed to fall asleep immediately.

"Oh, we can't stop," Mother exclaimed anxiously from the back seat. "We're already running late!" Only snoring noises came in answer from Dad. Mother shook her head and let out a long sigh of exasperation. She had never learned to drive but was aware that fourteen-year-old Mary Anna had been driving Dad about the ranch for some time and had even secretly driven him to town several times.

Now that Dad was soundly asleep, Mary Anna began making a logical, determined, utterly persuasive argument that since we were running late, she could certainly take over and drive this car down this new road that ran straight as an arrow and had no traffic. Even if she drove slowly, a lot less time would be lost by our moving than if we just sat here stopped on the side of the road while Dad had his greatly needed nap. He probably would be ready to drive again soon and we still might get there on time if we went on now.

Mother, in the parked and hot car, looked at her watch, fanning her flushed face with the road map, and thought it over. Mary Anna's argument did make sense. We really were running late, it was a wide, new, straight road with no traffic, and Dad was obviously not going to be able to drive until he had a nap. Finally, Mother gave in and said maybe it would be all right letting Mary Anna drive for a little while as Dad finished his needed siesta.

Dad was shaken awake and apprised of this new plan. He gave no objections; really he seemed mainly interested in continuing his nap. So he got into the back seat with Mother, and a grinning Mary Anna slid behind the wheel. I remained in the copilot's position in the front seat.

Dad immediately resumed his nap while Mother sat up straight and alert beside him. Mary Anna pulled the big Roadmaster Buick out onto the new highway and we were on our way. Under Mother's watchful eye, Mary Anna was the last word of a conservative, safety-conscious driver as we bumbled sedately down the wide, empty straight highway at a staid thirty-five miles an hour.

Mile after weary mile crawled by. Mother's eyelids began to lower. After jerking herself awake several times, she gave up the fight and leaned her head over to pillow it against her sleeping husband's shoulder and joined him in deep slumber.

We both glanced back at our soundly sleeping parents in the back seat. Mary Anna hissed, "You watch the speedometer," as she took deadly aim down the long, straight highway and, as the old saying goes, "really stuck her foot in the carburetor."

The Roadmaster Buick, considered the fastest stock car in the nation, instantly responded to the new tempo. The sound of the engine changed from the smooth, docile drone we were accustomed to and instead began to make an awesome, deep roaring, wild sound. I stared at the speedometer, transfixed, incredulous as the needle swept smoothly across the dial. This was one of the first ordinary cars to have a speedometer whose numbers didn't stop at one hundred but went on to 120. I had never, ever imagined those higher numbers to be functional, but it now seemed they would actually soon be needed as the car continued to accelerate far beyond my expectations.

Before long, the line of fence posts along the highway began to resemble a picket fence while the spacing of the telephone poles began to resemble a line of fence posts. Our tires, crossing the expansion joints of the concrete slabs, began to sound like we were continuously crossing a cattle guard.

I ceased to breathe as the speedometer needle continued moving past one hundred. Even Mary Anna began to look somewhat scared—but not very. 105, 106, 110.

"She's floorboarded," Mary Anna excitedly whispered. I found no reason to doubt it. The needle slowly leveled off and settled just short of 120, about 117, I decided. We were simply streaking across the desert on the new highway with our sleeping parents blissfully unaware in the back seat.

Suddenly a problem arose. Coming toward us through the shimmering heat waves ahead was an approaching car. The two cars, headed in different directions, whizzed past each other. The rate of closure had been so terrific, our eyes had little time to adjust, but it was painfully and sickeningly obvious to us that the other car had been a black Ford, with the front doors painted white and bearing the gold shield of the Texas Highway Patrol.

Horrified, I wheeled around and looked over the heads of our still sleeping, unaware parents in the back seat. Through the back window, I beheld the fast receding black Ford careening wildly back and forth over the highway. I couldn't decide if its erratic behavior was due to the driver attempting to stop and turn around or if it was just a reaction to being caught in our jet stream and almost blown off the road. As we were moving away rapidly, I didn't have to wonder long. My last impression was that the black Ford was either turning around or turning over. Whatever, we soon were out of sight, for

Mary Anna never did let up on the accelerator for an instant but kept it firmly "floorboarded."

I continued to watch fearfully out the back window while we whizzed along but could see nothing in the way of a pursuing car behind us. Quite a while later, the patrol car still wasn't in sight was we flashed by a yellow sign that said "Welcome to New Mexico—The Land of Enchantment." We were certainly enchanted to be there.

There was little communication back then between police vehicles. Two-way radios were very rare and cell phones nonexistent, so after entering New Mexico we began to relax and feel reasonably secure. Mary Anna let out a "whew" and let up on the gas pedal to let the car slow down since the New Mexico road was not nearly as good and smooth as the new Texas concrete highway had been.

When Mother and Dad finally began to stir and wake up from their naps, we were once again just bumbling along in a slow, sedate pace coming into Carlsbad, New Mexico. Dad told Mary Anna to turn into a filling station to fill up and let him resume driving. When we stopped, Dad got out, stretched mightily and then pulled out and looked at his watch. He and Mother got into an argument about what time we had left Pecos. Mother tartly reminded him that we gained an hour when we entered New Mexico and changed from Central Time to Mountain Time, but Dad continued to stare at his watch and look puzzled.

Mary Anna got in the back seat and became completely engrossed in reading a magazine she had already read twice. As for me, I kept staring south down the highway toward the Texas state line, fully expecting to see a long convoy of black-and-white Ford cars with sirens blaring, racing toward us. But all was serene.

After our visit with "the boys" at the Parent Day festivities, Mary Anna insisted that we go back home by Brownfield for "a change of scenery" instead of retracing our steps the way we had come by Pecos, so that is what we did.

We only got stuck three times.

Published by permission of Nancy Green.

During his rookie season in the National Football League in 1937, West Texan Sam Baugh played quarterback, defensive back, and punter for the Washington Redskins and led them to the NFL championship game (what would eventually become the Super Bowl) against the powerful Chicago Bears. Joe Holley picks up the action as the prologue to his biography of *Slingin' Sam: The Greatest Quarterback Ever to Play the Game.*

# Slingin' Sam

Joe Holley

Chicago. A dreary December afternoon so cold that anyone who dares to venture out runs the risk of frostbite, or worse. A punishing wind off frozen Lake Michigan only adds to the misery. The city is shut down, closed up, as Chicagoans seek warmth behind closed doors and boarded-up windows.

On the North Side, though, home to Wrigley Field, some fifteen thousand football fans have braved the dangerous conditions to watch a game, a National Football

League championship game between the fearsome Chicago Bears and the upstart Washington Redskins. Swaddled in layered coats and mufflers, wearing gloves, hats pulled down over their ears, these fans are fanatics in every sense of the word. Some caught the elevated train and rode it through a desolate downtown, the train winding its way through the canyon of tall buildings blocking out a pallid sun. Others rode streetcars past mounds of snow shoved out of roadways. Still others maneuvered Model Ts slowly and carefully through the icy streets.

The locals have come to see their Bears, the "Monsters of the Midway," a team of hard-nosed, big-shouldered brawlers who not only defeat their opponents almost every Sunday but also punish them in the process. Chicagoans like to think that the Bears of George Halas and Bronko Nagurski and George Musso truly embody their big, tough, hog-butcher-to-the-world metropolis.

Several thousand fans are there from out of town. They boarded a special train in Washington's Union Station and headed west. Disembarking at Chicago's LaSalle Street Station, fortified against the cold by flasks of alcohol stashed away in their overcoats, they hailed cabs to take them to the tidy brick ballpark that baseball's Chicago Cubs have made famous. Their Redskins are completing their first season in Washington, but already the capital city has taken them to its heart.

Years later, the NFL championship game will be called the Super Bowl. Years later, millions of football fans around the world will gather in front of their television sets to witness the spectacle. Advertisers will pay millions for a few minutes of viewing-audience time. On this cold day in Chicago, fewer than twenty thousand football fans, their very sanity in question, are on hand to witness one of the pivotal games in NFL history.

Shortly after noon, the two teams take the field for the kickoff, the Bears in their dark-blue jerseys trimmed in orange, the Redskins wearing their trademark burgundy and gold. Both teams wear tennis shoes, hoping to get whatever purchase they can on the ice-encrusted field. Mist from their breathing is visible in the frigid air.

The tall, spindly-legged Texan who ambles onto the frozen turf of Wrigley Field on that dreary Sunday afternoon has played in miserable weather before. The pride of Sweetwater, Texas, he has known northers that barrel across the plains with little warning, straight from the Canadian Arctic. As a high school senior four years earlier, he played in a blizzard, with driving snow and sleet pelting players and fans alike. But he has never played in temperatures so frigid that it hurts to breathe, so cold that hands and fingers ache and barely move, so cold that it is actually dangerous to be outdoors. He has never played on turf so hard and brittle that it rips bare skin like a cheese grater whenever someone hits the ground.

Backed up against his own goal line the first time the Redskins get the ball, young Sam Baugh looks around the huddle, ten men snorting steam in the punishing cold. He glances over the helmeted heads of his teammates, sees the mob of blue-shirted Bears waiting impatiently at the line of scrimmage to tear him apart. Literally. That is their game plan—hurt him any way they can, send him to the sidelines, knock him out of the game.

The Bears know he is special; so do his Redskin teammates. From the moment he rifled a bullet pass to a teammate in the team's first scrimmage—"Which eye, Coach?"—the Redskins knew they had something. And now, four months later, their confidence has been confirmed.

Although he is barely out of college, he has gained his teammates' respect during the long season, a season that has culminated in this moment, this championship game. They wait for his instructions. He glances over at Riley Smith, the Redskins' signal caller. (Sam is actually the tailback in the Redskins' single-wing formation.) Smith hears him out.

"Let's trick 'em," he suggests in his Texas drawl. "I'll drop into punt formation. But I won't punt." He glances at stellar running back Cliff Battles. "See that chunk of ice right over there?" he says, nodding toward a white spot on the yellowed grass. "Run straight to it, cut to the sideline and look for the ball."

The Redskins break their huddle and line up in punt formation. The Bears aren't surprised, since punting on first down is standard strategy when a team finds itself bottled up in its own end of the field. The Bears know that Sam is also one of the best punters in the game, possibly the best.

Smith calls the signals and Sam waits for the snap, his face beneath the leather helmet red and raw. His cold hands receive the ball, but instead of stepping into it with his strong right leg, he wraps his long fingers around it, feeling for the laces as he rolls to the right behind the goal line and looks downfield for Battles. The Redskin running back, running as fast as he can on the frozen field, carefully sets his pivot foot and cuts in front of a Bear safety, Gene Ronzani. As Ronzani slips on the ice, the Redskin halfback gathers in the Baugh toss over his right shoulder and motors up the sideline for a forty-two-yard gain.

Although the Bears hold shortly afterward, the pass from the end zone delivers a message: the Redskins' brilliant young passer isn't going to allow the elements to dictate strategy. Neither the weather nor the fearsome Bears can scare him.

*Editor's Note: Washington went on to win the game 28-21, with Baugh passing for three touchdowns in the second half. He and his twenty-two teammates each received a $234.26 payout.*

From *Slingin' Sam: The Life and Times of the Greatest Quarterback Ever to Play the Game* by Joe Holley, Copyright 2012, reprinted by permission of the University of Texas Press.

For more than twenty years, Nellie Witt Spikes wrote a newspaper column, As a Farm Woman Thinks, for several West Texas weeklies in and around Crosby County, east of Lubbock—from 1937, when she was 49, until 1960. Selections from those columns were collected into a delightful book edited by Geoff Cunfer and published by Texas Tech University Press under the title *As a Farm Woman Thinks.* The following piece is dated February 20, 1941.

# A West Texas Sandstorm

Nellie Witt Spikes

A West Texas sandstorm with all the trimmings is on. We only sigh as sand covers our pretty curtains, piles up under the doors and windows. We turn the radio on, only to hear maniacal shrieks. Turn it off and wish the mail would come.

Russian thistles pile in the gates and under clotheslines and on back porches, their favorite haunts. They stick our fingers with fine briers as we try to push them out of the doorways.

Scared-looking gray clouds come over and it is dark; we turn on the electric lights; the wind has blown out a fuse. Our hands get sewing dirty, we lay it aside. We look at one another; why, we must all have the yaller janders, we are so yellow and ghastly looking.

We fix a little lunch, have to wash out the dishes we use before we eat. Dirt makes patterns in the sink and bathtub. We forget to cover the separator. It will have to be washed before it is used.

The whistling wind never ceases. Small pebbles and dirt hit our faces if we dare venture outside. Passing cars creep along with lights dimmed from the sand.

Why don't we leave? Well, stranger, we all plan to have our minds fully made up by the time the wind ceases.

But the next day we sweep the dirt up into shovels, dust off the enlarged pictures of Pa and Ma, put the beds out to sun, and listen to the radio while we work. When all is done, the house clean, the fresh-smelling quilts brought in, a pot of red beans simmering on the stove, and fresh-ironed clothes hung up, somehow we forget our resolve made while the sandstorm raged.

The plains have days so promising. Days of mellow sunshine and cool, soft winds. A wonderful year is just ahead of you, she murmurs in our willing ears. Just stay, silver slanting rains will sweep over the prairie, blades of maize will look like cool, clear water as they wave; cotton will bloom and turn to fields of snow. Don't leave me, she urges, you could never forget the good, clear water in such never-failing abundance, nights in the summer you will not turn over and over, sleepless from the heat.

"I promise you," the plains plays over and over on her mighty stringed instrument—the wind.

From *As a Farm Woman Thinks: Life and Land on the Texas High Plains, 1890–1960*, by Nellie Witt Spikes, edited by Geoff Cunfer. Copyright © 2010 by Geoff Cunfer. Reprinted with the permission of The Permissions Company, Inc., on behalf of Texas Tech University Press (ttuppress.org).

Dick Tarpley began his newspaper career as a reporter in Wichita Falls and concluded it as editor and columnist in Abilene. In his book, *A Rush of Memories*, Tarpley recalled one crime story in particular that involved both cities in the early 1940s.

# The Paper Sack Bandit

Dick Tarpley

The slight, nice-looking nineteen-year-old had terrorized bankers, druggists, and store clerks for a year or more.

He became known as the "paper sack bandit" because he always brought two guns and a paper sack with him in each of the dozens of holdups from Wichita Falls to Abilene and from Amarillo to Dallas. He'd hand the paper sack to the clerk or teller and quietly tell them to "put all your money in the sack and hand it back."

His cool demeanor, his self-assurance, his dominance of the scene, despite his 130-pound frame, commanded obedience. The message seemed clear. Bravado on the part of the clerk could prove deadly.

He never fired a gun in a holdup. He never had to. Clerks did exactly as he told them. He always walked casually out of the bank or the store, then another two to four blocks to his parked car. He'd put the loot in the car, then amble down to the nearest theater and watch a show.

He collected thousands of dollars from banks at Stamford and Nocona, from the Hilton Hotel Drug Store in Abilene, from at least ten hijackings in Wichita Falls, and from other stickups in North and Northwest Texas.

He never wore a mask but somehow thought he was immune to identification. He seemingly flaunted capture both in his holdups and in his daily habits, though he carefully avoided using stolen cars, usually driving his own, and generally moved from town to town after robberies.

But he played the same cities once too often. He ordered a hot dog in a Wichita Falls restaurant shortly after his nineteenth birthday. An usher from the Majestic Theater, which the young bandit had robbed a short time before, recognized him and called police.

Detective Gene Brown arrested Rex Beard Jr. in the café. As they reached the door, Beard ran. Brown shot once, wounding the youth in the arm but not stopping him. Police found him four blocks away, trying to open the trunk of his car. They realized the significance of the arrest when the car yielded several guns, ammunition, and thousands of dollars in the glove compartment.

The Hilton holdup brought a twenty-five-year sentence, with similar punishment for other crimes in Stamford, Wichita Falls, Vernon, and Montague. Federal authorities had him returned to Abilene from Vernon to face prosecution for the national bank holdups.

While in jail in Abilene, Beard paid a twenty-year-old soldier, home from Fort Bliss on leave and visiting a friend in the next cell, fifteen dollars to buy a pistol and promised $155 more if he would bring it back to him on a second visit to the friend. The soldier complied, saying later that Beard had promised not to fire it during his escape. That $170 transaction eventually would cost the soldier two years in state prison.

About 8 P.M. on February 12, 1942, Deputy Sheriff Wade Willis, a forty-nine-year-old former barber known as the "singing deputy," accompanied Jailer Jess Edwards to the second floor of the jail to get Beard and bring him downstairs to await federal officials, who were to move him to Dallas. Per jail policy, neither wore guns.

When Beard left the cell, he pulled the smuggled gun and said, "Stick 'em up."

Willis slashed the young bandit across the wrist with the heavy leather strap he had intended to use as a shackle. Beard shot once, striking Willis in the heart. It was the only shot proven to be fired in anger by young Beard, but it would send him to the electric chair.

Edwards ran down the inside stairs to the basement, with Beard in pursuit. Edwards flipped off the lights and then fled out a basement door, closing it behind him and trapping the escapee.

Thirty or forty law enforcement officers surrounded the jail. Sheriff Sid McAdams and Police Chief T. A. Hackney entered the jail and fired a hail of bullets at Beard as he ran up the stairs. He had dropped the gun in the basement, but the officers did not know it. Beard crumpled to the floor, critically wounded in the lungs and liver and with both arms broken.

Surgeons saved his life—temporarily. A little over a year later, he was convicted of murder by a Fisher County jury in Roby. (The case was moved from Abilene because of publicity and public anger.) After the customary appeals failed, District Judge Owen Thomas sentenced him to die.

One month later, on September 3, 1943, at 12:10 A.M., the saga of the super-calm, cocky little "paper sack bandit" ended. Old Sparky claimed another victim before a small audience at the Huntsville penitentiary.

From *A Rush of Memories* by Dick Tarpley, reprinted by permission of Beverly Tarpley and the *Abilene Reporter-News*.

The Women Airforce Service Pilots trained in Sweetwater during World War II, forever changing the role of women in aviation. WASP Museum Associate Director Carol Cain tells their story.

# Women Airforce Service Pilots

Carol Cain

Sweetwater's Avenger Field became the first and only all-female flight training base in U.S. military history when the Women Airforce Service Pilots (WASP) moved their facility from Houston to Sweetwater in May 1943.

The history of these aviation pioneers is more exciting, emotional, and inspirational than any work of fiction.

From the fall of 1942 through December 1944, 1,830 women pilots—ages eighteen to thirty-five, possessing a private or commercial pilot's license—answered the call of their country and joined the WASP. Though they never left continental North America, the contributions of the 1,074 who graduated, received their wings at

Avenger Field, and were deployed to 126 bases all over the United States, helped turn the tide in favor of America and our Allies.

They came from all walks of life. Many left children, families, college, and careers. Some had fathers, brothers, fiancés, or boyfriends who were already in the service. Paying their own way, picking up other trainees along the way, they came to Sweetwater by train, bus, or family automobile. One girl flew her private plane when reporting for duty. Despite their diversity, their passion for aviation fueled their desire to fly the powerful aircraft that were being developed for the war effort.

From the standpoint of skills, ability, and experience, the WASP were an elite corps—but also guinea pigs. No program like this had ever been tried before. Jackie Cochran realized the future of women in military aviation hung on how these women performed professionally and conducted themselves morally and socially.

Although they maintained military standards and observed military regulations, they were Civil Service. Their first uniforms were mechanics coveralls—size 44. A $172.50 monthly salary had to cover room and board plus dress uniforms, laundry and transportation. Two six-girl bays shared a latrine with two showers, two sinks, and two toilets that had been built for men.

The young women gladly endured these hardships to meet the objectives of the program: to relieve male pilots for combat, determine if women could serve as military pilots, and decrease the demand on the Air Force's manpower pools.

Even though the women already knew how to fly, they were sent to Sweetwater to learn to fly the Army way—under the direction of Jacqueline Cochran and General Hap Arnold.

After graduation, their assignments included ferrying planes from factories to bases, towing targets for live ammunition ground/aerial gunnery practice, and serving as test pilots for repaired aircraft (sent to the U.S. from the front).

In Sweetwater they trained in basic, primary, and advanced single- and double-engine aircraft. They went on to more advanced pilot training flying high-powered fighter and bomber aircraft, including the B-17 and B-29. Of the seventy-seven types of planes in the Army Air Corps arsenal, a WASP flew each of them.

Training at Avenger Field lasted thirty weeks. The 393 hours of ground school included math, physics, maps, charts, navigation, weather, communication, Morse code, first aid, and other topics. The 210 hours of flight training included primary, basic, instrument, advanced, and multi-engine. About half of each day was spent in class and half spent flying.

On weekends, local ranchers put on ranch rodeos for those girls from the east who wanted to experience cowboy life. One local family opened its cabin on Lake Sweetwater to the WASP every Sunday for fried chicken and homemade ice cream.

When some citizens complained about all the "new people" in town, the government started paying the WASP with $2 bills—and the business community soon saw the positive impact of the WASP program.

Because the WASP were paid under Civil Service and not part of the military, they received no military benefits or insurance. They had to pay their way to Avenger Field and their way home when the program was deactivated.

Thirty-eight WASP were killed in service to their country, but they could have no American flag on their coffins, they could not be buried in military cemeteries, and their families could place no star in their windows.

Although the program was a success, political maneuvering led to its deactivation on December 20, 1944. Grueling schedules, sacrifices, gender bias and the loss of thirty-eight women pilots apparently meant nothing. Their records were sealed and they were asked not to talk about their training. These well-trained and capable women were expected to go home and assume their proper place in post-war society.

Many of the WASP returned to families and careers —and many maintained flying as a hobby. Yet there were some who enlisted in other branches of the service or pursued careers in aviation as private pilots, design engineers, or in control towers.

TWA countered the disbanded WASP applications for pilot positions with job offers as stewardesses. One WASP replied; "I'm not going to serve coffee in the back of a plane knowing that I'm a better pilot than the guy in the cockpit."

In the 1970s, as military institutions were opening their doors to women, the U.S. Navy announced that it was training women cadets to fly—"the first women to fly military aircraft"—ignoring the WASP program.

After being denied military status by the U.S. House of Representatives in 1944, the WASP petitioned Washington, and with the help of Sen. Barry Goldwater, finally received military status recognition in 1977.

In 2010, the Woman Airforce Service Pilots received the Congressional Gold Medal from President Barack Obama. The Congressional Gold Medal is awarded to persons "who have performed an achievement that has an impact on American history and culture that is likely to be recognized as a major achievement in the recipient's field long after the achievement." More than three hundred WASP and WASP family members were in Washington to accept this long overdue honor.

In 2002, WASP were granted the right to be buried in Arlington National Cemetery and other military cemeteries. The right to be inurned in Arlington National Cemetery was withdrawn in 2015 by the outgoing Secretary of the Army, but not without public outrage, and the decision is under challenge in both the House and Senate, with backing from congressional, military, aviation, and public supporters.*

Although the WASP were left out of American history textbooks, denied rights, given inferior equipment, and subjected to gender bias, their story is now being told. The young women who fly today's advanced military aircraft give credit to the WASP for paving the way for them to follow their own dream of flying.

In 2005, the National WASP World War II Museum opened in Sweetwater overlooking the runways where they received military flight training. It is open to the public Wednesday through Saturday from 10 A.M. to 5 P.M. and Sunday 1 to 5 P.M. Admission is free.

At this writing early in 2016, there are 117 surviving WASP—the youngest is ninety-one and two are 103. These ladies are as interesting and possess the same spirit of adventure they had when they were in service. At one WASP's one-hundredth birthday, a sister WASP, who was ninety, walked up to her and said, "Happy Birthday—I'm here to see how I'll look in ten years."

Every year the WASP return to Avenger Field the Saturday before Memorial Day to reconnect with old friends. Some are on walkers or in wheelchairs, but each has her own military escort for the day.

In interviews most have said, "Those were the best days of our lives." One commented, "We would have flown for free if they had let us."

Today as the sun sets over Hangar One, if you are very quiet you can hear the echoes of the WASP singing their marching songs on hallowed ground.

**Editor's note: In a bipartisan effort, Congress passed legislation that was signed into law by President Obama on May 20, 2016, giving WASP members the right to be inurned in Arlington National Cemetery.*

Published with permission of the author.

In his book *Chance Encounters*, A. C. Greene tells about the first time he saw Lyndon Johnson on the campaign trail.

# LBJ's Hat Is in the Ring

A. C. Greene

In the summer of 1948, fresh out of college, I went to work for the *Abilene Reporter-News.* I'd never seen Congressman Lyndon Baines Johnson, so I was delighted when the paper's political writer invited me to drive with him to Anson, the county seat of Jones, the next county.

Johnson was to visit by way of helicopter. The use of a helicopter was a campaign first in Texas. If this were an ordinary campaign for senator, there wouldn't be any point in Lyndon Johnson flying around the state, appearing at little towns like Anson (population 2,700) in West Texas, which was not his political home turf.

But running against Coke Stevenson, Johnson was going to need every scrap of vote he could get. Coke

Stevenson had been a popular wartime governor of Texas, the portrait of "Old Mr. Texas": a tall, slender (very successful!) rancher, rugged with honesty, uprightness written all over his tanned, mature face—the stereotype of a senator from the Great Southwest.

Congressman Johnson was seen by a lot of Texas Democrats as being "too Washington," too ambitious and too sly (this was when winning the Texas Democratic runoff was tantamount to election). He'd been Franklin Roosevelt's hand-picked boy—but Roosevelt was dead.

Coke Stevenson had been drafted out of retirement to run against Johnson and was conducting a strong campaign. Johnson's political life was on the line. He'd lost to W. Lee O'Daniel in the same Senate race in 1942 and if Stevenson defeated him now Johnson might (with luck) remain a congressman, but nothing more.

I was as much interested in the helicopter as I was the candidate; helicopters were a rare species of bird, having been introduced only toward the end of World War II. Johnson had staged a political coup by engaging the helicopter with which to campaign.

The political writer and I got to Anson ahead of time, parking on the edge of the vacant field where the helicopter was to come to earth. When it appeared, some thirty or so minutes late (politicians are always late) everyone was peering skyward, captured by the sight of this dragonfly of the air that hovered, with a great whoosh, and was gently descending straight down.

Suddenly, a voice boomed out, the voice of God, speaking from heaven, catching us off guard: "My fellow Texans . . . this is your next senator, Lyndon Johnson." Then, when the helicopter was about ten feet off the ground, a door suddenly opened from which a white, ten-gallon hat came flying, along with another booming announcement: "My hat is in the ring!"

The instant the helicopter touched the ground, Lyndon Johnson leaped out, retrieved his hat, jammed it on his head and began pressing the flesh (as he liked to call it). He moved quickly, looking into the eyes of each person as he shook his or her hand. The political writer told me, afterward, that the first hand Johnson had grabbed was that of the Jones County Republican chairman, and LBJ was in such a hurry the County Democratic chairman and the Anson mayor (Democrat) couldn't catch up with him.

I was amused to see the candidate pressing the flesh of a Mexican-American cotton picker who had come running from a nearby patch and was grinning delightedly, chattering away in machine gun Spanish. He was reluctant to let go of Johnson's hand, following the candidate along, but I caught the phrase *"el presidente!"* a couple of times, so that helped.

With a waving, embracing gesture to the crowd, the candidate climbed back in the helicopter (that had never cut its engines) and it rose majestically into the blue. The crowd, which had stood startled and stunned when he was among them, suddenly gave a cheer toward the disappearing bird: LBJ all the way!

Lyndon Johnson won the election by only eighty-seven votes, after a recount, and those eighty-seven were bitterly contested from Texas to the Supreme Court. But voter lists and election boxes mysteriously disappeared and the Supreme Court ruled it had no jurisdiction over the state election.

It was the tightest U.S. Senate race in American history. And it took nearly two decades for Lyndon Johnson to outlive the sneering nickname, "Landslide Lyndon."

From *Chance Encounters* by A. C. Greene, reprinted by permission of the A. C. Greene Estate.

Burle Pettit, editor emeritus of the *Lubbock Avalanche-Journal*, reflects on the simple pleasures he recalls growing up in Moran.

# Simple Pleasures

Burle Pettit

While driving over to pick up an ice cream freezer I saw advertised in my favorite newspaper, I wondered how much, if any, it would resemble the one that played such a delightful role in making my childhood worth remembering.

I couldn't tell much by the picture in the ad but the one plucked from my memory was as clear as the day playing out before me.

In it, the freezer can was housed inside a large oaken bucket, which was as imposing as the anticipation it aroused. Few things excited my boyhood imagination like the thoughts of making ice cream.

With the throes of the Great Depression still lingering and the inevitability of a world war looming, those were times when rural people were as plain as the earth that sustained them. Simple pleasures were the only pleasures and, for that reason, they never seemed simple at all.

Rural Texans of those times took frivolity where they could find it. Other than occasional hayrides, barn dances, box suppers, and taffy pulls, entertainment was generally confined to the home.

Being the youngest of the six kids that made up our family, my latitude was often limited by the whims of my three brothers. For example, we had in the pasture behind our two-story, Walton-type house, a stock pond complete with diving board. I could not go near it to swim—or even to catch crawfish—without a brother along. Made no sense to me because I had learned to swim the summer of my fourth birthday.

On the east side of our house stood a large, sprawling live oak tree that was my personal entertainment center. A swing hung from one of its lateral limbs and, up several branches higher, my brothers had built a tree house that was their own private hideout.

In a family of that size, my life never seemed dull. My older brothers gave me a lot of attention, most of which was good. One exception was the time I sneaked into their hideout and brought into the house half a plug of chewing tobacco and a partial sack of Bull Durham.

Suffice it to say siblings in such a large family have their own justice system.

Our special treats were often connected to a holiday, such as the Fourth of July, or on a Sunday afternoon following a Saturday trip into town.

Sometimes it was as simple as a watermelon feast which, at our house, was turned into a ritual, with Dad deciding on the method of distribution.

Often, he would cut them into individual slices; other times they would be cut in half, end to end, and we'd attack them with spoons, which became virtual épées in a duel for a bite of the heart, the sweetest part of the melon.

Following was the seed-spitting contest, where I really shined. I guarantee you, had there been a pro league for that venue, I would have been an early-round draft pick.

But the really special time for me was when Mom decided it was time to make a freezer of ice cream. The occasion was marked not only by the eating but the routine leading up to it.

Dad would unwrap the extra block of ice he'd picked up in town the day before. One had already been put into our non-electric icebox, where it served as the coolant. The other he would chip into chunks while Mom was formulating her special recipe for Homemade Ice Cream.

I capitalize it because hers was a brand to itself and would be illegal in any state where calories in excess of three thousand per spoonful were prohibited by law.

I do not remember her recipe but I do have vivid recollection of some of the contents, the principal one being real cream, separated by Mom from the cow's milk and used for churning butter and for Dad's coffee.

The freezing process was a ritual. My sis and I would take turns sitting on top of the freezer while my brothers switched off on the cranking. After what seemed forever, Dad would give it a final check and proclaim it ready to serve.

Soon I will look at my new freezer while recalling the boyhood model. And then it will dawn on me that it's not only the freezers I'm trying to compare but the times themselves.

Reprinted by permission of the author, from the *Lubbock Avalanche-Journal*, June 21, 2014.

Lynda Fogerson was born in Matador and now lives in Amarillo. She was a county extension agent in West Texas for twenty-five years. This piece on childhood obesity was published in 2013 in the *Abilene Reporter-News*.

# Childhood Obesity Wasn't a Problem Back Then

Lynda Fogerson

My granddaughter came to me a few years ago when everyone was at our home watching television and said, "Grammy, do you only have three TVs?"

I said, "Yes, Chase, but when I was growing up, I didn't have any TV." In wide-eyed wonder she asked, "What did you DO?"

Every time I see a media story about childhood obesity and all the health problems of today's young people, I am reminded of my answer to her. What I and most other children of my time did every day is the key to why childhood obesity was a rarity until recent years.

To a child today, no life existed before TVs, computers, DVDs, and cell phones. And, by the way, I also didn't have a phone in my home as a child.

So what did we do for entertainment without all the electronic gadgets today's children believe bring joy to their lives but result in a couch potato lifestyle and the resulting extra pounds and potential health problems?

We rode bicycles, climbed trees, and hung by our knees upside down from tree limbs and monkey bars, waded in the creek, crawled under the bridge, roamed through the pasture and got cactus thorns in our feet, which Mother had to pull out with pliers.

We climbed on the barns, made a playhouse in the chicken feed barn, hung bedspreads over the clothesline or windmill tower to make a playhouse. And we did all this while wearing dresses—the girls, that is.

We also played baseball with friends, had clod fights when the field was plowed, and made mud pies. I also had pet chickens, one of which laid a soft-shell egg in my lap once when I held her too long.

The main motivator, besides fun, was to get out of the house. Because, you see, most of us had mothers who were homemakers. If we got under foot, they would find a job for us to do. Mother would have us mop a floor, clean the chrome table and chair legs, wash the baseboards, iron or some other "unfun" chore. The threat of chores has an amazing ability to clear the room of kids! Most moms are not home all day now to pass out these chores.

Another contributor to obesity is the wealth of foods from takeout, fast-food restaurants, and supermarkets. Any food you can dream of, you can get with little effort.

When I was growing up, my mother grew and cooked all the food we ate. We never ate out except on a rare vacation.

But few children of that time had any weight problem. Just look in old school yearbooks. Why was that? Because when kids are active—physically—working and playing, they don't have time to graze all day. When they are watching TV or playing video games, the only exercise is to their fingers—pushing buttons and snacking on food.

After twenty-five years of teaching nutrition and watching my mother live almost ninety-seven years in amazingly good health, and never overweight, I am convinced that the lifestyle habits we have throughout our lives related to food and exercise have a strong correlation to the quality of life and health we have as older adults.

Parents who want to give their children the best of everything and deny them nothing, may be depriving them of the good old-fashioned opportunity to be active and creative through outdoor activities and unstructured play.

Be sure that while you are giving your children everything you didn't have as a child, you are giving them the good things you did have, like physical play and a healthy future.

Reprinted by permission of the author and the *Abilene Reporter-News*.

Elroy Bode taught school in El Paso for nearly half a century and is considered one of Texas's foremost essayists. This piece is from his book *In a Special Light*, published by Trinity University Press.

# Nobody Whistles Anymore

Elroy Bode

When I was growing up it seemed as if everybody whistled at one time or another. It was like breathing or smiling or saying hello. Or feeding the dog, watering the lawn, reading the newspaper in the front room. Whistling was a normal thing for people to do.

Kids whistled as they rode their bikes across a vacant lot. Garage mechanics whistled walking around the raised hood of a car they were working on. My grandmother whistled—not truly, not with a brisk shrillness, but breathily, softly, almost tunelessly, just to herself, as she moved about her ranch kitchen at ten o'clock in the morning getting the meal ready for dinnertime. High school boys whistled in self-assured confidence as they walked toward the front door of their date's house on Saturday night.

Postmen seemed to be the most spirited, most memorable whistlers in my home town. Mr. Michon was a short, wiry, red-faced man who seemed to thrive on carrying his mail pouch block after block—walking onto porches and paying no attention to the dogs behind screen doors or in the side yards, then walking back out into the brief shade of oaks and chinaberries—and all the while whistling to the morning, the sunshine, the town. He was regular as clockwork in every neighborhood, and his whistle always preceded him by half a block.

But something happened after I grew up. Whistling just seemed to die away. Maybe people became weighted down by serious concerns and felt they had no time to waste on trivial matters—but I don't believe that was really the reason. (Americans continued to whistle during the Depression, during World War II . . . )

As best I can figure, whistling began to disappear sometime in the 1960s—about the time that poetry began to shrivel up and die in public school classrooms; when Vietnam became our national preoccupation; when disaffected youth in blue jeans discovered drugs and racism and the various imperfections of their elders;

when Broadway show tunes and other romantic, melodic songs gave way to the grim expressions of social protest.

A person whistles when his psyche is in equilibrium, when there is a simplicity in his heart and a buoyancy in his soul. A person whistling in his car is like a bird tootling in a tree. Has the complexity of modern life rendered us incapable of joy in the morning and a sense of freedom in the afternoon? Is the inability to whistle an indictment of our present national character or just a negligible absence of something not very important anyway?

Maybe the topic is one for the scholars. Maybe we will have to wait for a Harvard sociologist—or any properly serious-minded fellow—to publish his dissertation, "Whistling: Its Origins and Ramifications as Reflected in the Psychoanalytically Oriented Studies of Multicultural Populations." I might read such a weighty treatise but—like my grandmother—I'll be whistling softly under my breath.

From *In a Special Light by* Elroy Bode, Copyright 2006 Elroy Bode, reprinted by permission of Trinity University Press (tupress.org).

Carlton Stowers, author of more than forty books, grew up in Ballinger and Abilene back in the days when horned toads were everywhere in West Texas.

# Confessions of a Horned Toad Hunter

Carlton Stowers

To characterize the summers of my youth as misspent would, I believe, be a tad harsh. Still, my field of vision when twelve-going-on-thirteen was limited to anticipation of the next Little League game and what Saturday afternoon shoot-'em-up would be shown at the downtown Texas Theater. I could not have spelled "ecology," much less defined it. The importance of maintaining a balance of nature and the concept of protecting the environment? I didn't have a clue.

And so, all these years later, a bit more aware, I come to apologize; to confess that I'm the guy who thoughtlessly aided the disappearance of one of nature's grand creatures from the landscape of my southwest. Wonder why you don't see the little prehistoric-looking Texas horned lizard anymore? I'm the guy to blame.

Time was when the arid West Texas terrain was the free-ranging home to the hand-size creature the scientists called the *Phyrnosoma cornutum.* Those of us less academically bent referred to them as horned toads—or horny toads—because of the devilish horns on their foreheads and along their spines. They were as much a part of rural Texas as barbecue and country music.

Over in Eastland, the legend was that the city fathers placed one in the time capsule cornerstone of a newly built courthouse back in 1897 and when, thirty-one years later, it was opened, the little guy, who they quickly named Old Rip, was still alive. He was taken on a national tour, even stopping in at the White House to visit President Calvin Coolidge.

No wonder the fascinating little lizard was long ago designated the official state reptile. Even today visitors to the Southwest Texas community of Kenedy are greeted by a highway sign proclaiming it the Horned Lizard Capital of Texas. Texas Christian University in Fort Worth adopted the Horned Frog as its athletic mascot, and the late Dr. June Welch, in his 1993 book *O*

*Ye Legendary Texas Horned Frog!*, took note of the formation of a Horned Lizard Conservation Society.

As late as the mid 1950s, all one needed to do was check out the nearest red ant bed to find horned toads lurking nearby, capturing the insects with their spear-like tongues. And there was a time when I knew the location of every feeding place within miles of my Runnels County home. That was the summer of my venture as an adolescent entrepreneur.

I had somehow obtained the mailing address of a Topeka, Kansas, curio shop that was willing to pay ten cents for each horned toad I could ship their way. It was my understanding that kids who frequented their store overwhelmingly preferred them over goldfish or baby turtles as bedroom pets.

Finances were a bit slim back then, and it wasn't always easy to scrape up the dime admission to the picture show. Thus I spent long summer days as a tireless hunter, daily visiting vacant lots and back alleys, chasing down horned toads, which I would then place in one of Mom's washtubs that sat on the back porch. When I had collected enough to fill a shoe box (carefully punctured with air holes, mind you), I proudly marched to the post office, mailed them away and anxiously awaited the payment that would soon arrive.

My buddies, aware of the gold mine I'd hit upon, pled to know the address of my Kansas connection. While I kept it a carefully guarded secret, I did reach a free enterprise agreement whereby I began paying three cents for every horned toad they brought to me. Business boomed. That summer I had money to burn.

And, alas, the seemingly endless local horned toad population was greatly diminished. My bid for celestial wealth lasted but one fleeting summer since I somehow lost my benefactor's address. Soon, others involved in horned toad trafficking would suffer the same fate. In 1960, the Texas legislature passed a law forbidding shipping the little reptiles out of state.

A half century later, Oklahoma City filmmaker Stefanie Leland produced a documentary titled "Where Has the Horny Toad Gone?" According to her research, the decline of the species can be blamed on multiple culprits: urban development, the arrival of deadly fire ants which killed off the larger red ants and numerous other Texas insects that were part of the horned toads' diet, and the extensive use of pesticides. And, of course, what she refers to as the "pet trade" in which I was a guilty participant.

"Actually," said Leland, "it is a bit of a mystery. There doesn't seem to be any one single cause for their disappearance." But, there's no question they've become a rarity. In Kenedy, which still proclaims itself the Horned Toad Capital, no one's actually seen one in several years.

Which saddens me. Today I can only offer this *mea culpa* for the part I played. If I had it to do over again, I'd let the majestic little creatures run free and instead seek my fortune redeeming discarded soda pop bottles.

Published by permission of the author.

Jay Moore grew up in Abilene and is the city's foremost historian. He teaches at Abilene High School and has produced books and DVDs on Abilene history.

# A Marker for Dixie Lee

Jay Moore

It was after my grandmother died I realized just how deeply her lack of education embarrassed her. It was a secret shame she carried; a shame I totally missed while she was alive. In the time I knew her, she was always older than fifty and lived in a big house and drove a new Cadillac and maneuvered fine through the chores of daily life.

In the knotty-pine paneled den there were bookshelves and many hardback books, including a set of *Encyclopedia Britannica* I often leafed through. It was the room she used the most—watching her soaps, crocheting, working a puzzle, visiting. But I never saw her with one of the books in her lap.

Following her death, my dad, her son, came to own the contents of those bookshelves and so I sat down to look over the books and see if there were any I might add to my own shelves. The first book I picked up was the historical fiction of Catherine Marshall titled *Christy.* On the first page I saw in my grandmother's familiar handwriting, *This is one of the best books I have read.*

For that reason alone I thought I might like to read it as well and began a stack to take to my car. Picking up another, I noticed the same handwritten notation in a '50s-era novel. Ditto for the third and fourth book and nearly all the rest. It seemed odd that she would record such thoughts as though she might one day pick the book up again and be reminded that it was a worthy read.

It slowly dawned: She was not writing introspective analyses nor trying to convey the quality to a future reader who might pluck the book from her shelf. Rather, she wrote comments in the front of books she never read because she could never read. The stigma of an elementary level education shamed her to write epithets in books to throw others off the scent.

When Granny—a name that truly didn't fit her—was fourteen she took a trip from her home near Waco to visit the family of her uncle in Runnels County, Texas. On that trip, she met a neighbor of her relatives who was nine years older and who would become my grandfather. The following fall they were married. She was fifteen, and he was twenty-four. They lived in a two-room board-and-batten house that my granddad built on some land his parents had given him to farm.

It was in that house that Granny gave birth at age sixteen. I never knew if a doctor, or even a neighbor, was available to help with the birth but, in the end, the baby girl was dead. A small box was found to serve as a coffin and Grandaddy, alone, took the wooden box to the cemetery east of Winters, Texas. He placed her in the earth next to another infant, his own infant brother who died at birth as well. He buried his daughter to the side of his brother.

Sixteen is young to be a mother, much less one who is grieving. I've wondered just how my grandmother coped inside that slim home. By the time she was eighteen she had a healthy baby boy, followed by five more boys.

We were often at Granny and Grandaddy's home. The upstairs room at the end of the hall was Grandaddy's office. On the wall was a large, framed family tree a draftsman friend had drawn upon Grandaddy's instructions. The tree trunk was Granny and Grandaddy and it was comforting to see the generations diagrammed in the logic of family connections. Sons were branches and my dad was near the tree's middle. But the low, first branch was the intriguing one to me. It was a short branch that was labeled "infant."

Grandaddy died in 1985 and within a short time Granny's sons had convinced her to sell the home she had lived in for thirty-five years and disseminate the furniture and dishes and family tree. She moved to a smaller house before boxing all up and moving to a nursing home when she was eighty-five.

During those days of her living in just one room with commercial furniture and a view of an empty field, I would stop by and visit several times each week. Granny and I had many conversations—some short, some long enough that they ended with her falling asleep. We discussed family and church and the news. She enjoyed the microwave hamburgers you could buy from a machine down the hall, and I often was sent with quarters to make the purchase and do the zapping, adding mustard and ketchup from the small packets next to the microwave.

I don't recall how it was that on one visit we talked about the family tree and the lowest branch. Granny told me the story of the unnamed baby girl and the burial and the difficult days. She bemoaned having never visited the grave and she was not even sure of the name of the cemetery and only vaguely familiar with its location east of Winters. She knew a woman still living in Winters who would know, and I sensed she was asking me to go on a mission for her, a mission much more important than my trips down the hall to the vending machine.

That is how I came to drive forty miles south to pick up Leona Billups one day at her small home in Winters. She had known my grandparents for most of her life and understood their early life story better than I did. We drove east on a farm-to-market road and she told me of the one-time community known as Truett that was named for Truett Billups, who had been a relation to her husband. The one-room-school community was long gone; the only remnant was the Truett Cemetery. The green sign pointing to Truett Cemetery was actually pointing at a gate into a farmer's field, and since the day was rainy we didn't venture farther.

I went to see Granny the next day and caught her up on Leona's life and her family. I told her that I knew the approximate location of the cemetery and that I would need to go back to open the gate and drive the rutted path. Granny told me that her infant daughter was buried beside the other baby, my granddad's brother, but she was not sure if that grave was marked.

On my second trip south, I took a friend. We arrived at the gate opposite the Truett Cemetery sign. I opened the gate and he drove the Suburban past so I could close it and keep cattle from escaping. We drove slowly through tall grass between tire ruts before coming to a second gate where I repeated the process. Soon we saw a fence at the end of the half-mile road. The fence surrounded a square plot of land with a wide silver gate that had welded metal letters spelling out TRUETT on top.

We parked and surveyed the overgrown plot that looked to be about three hundred feet square. Just inside the gate some headstones were visible, but others were far back among cactus and yuccas and grass that seemed prime real estate for snakes. We had not brought along hoes or shovels to hack at the growth or ward off reptiles.

I stepped in to begin a hunt for a headstone I was not sure even existed. The markers were spread far apart. There was no evidence of a row or path as in most cemeteries. At the far back corner of the property was a small tin-roofed building whose purpose was not obvious, but I gingerly stepped over cactus and cautiously examined the etched stones to see if there was one with my last name—Moore.

I used my heel to push over a yucca growing right next to a small stone. Behind the plant was a weathered inscription cut into the sandstone marker—"Infant son of D. S. and M. F. Moore"—Daniel Spurgeon and Mary Francis, my great-grandparents. My granddad's brother. A smile of relief came, for there behind the yucca was the spot where a young father laid his daughter more than seventy years ago. On one side or the other was Granny's daughter.

The next day, seated by her bed, I watched her face register a strange relief. A now eighty-seven-year-old mother who had never forgotten a daughter who never breathed life. Granny had discovered a child she'd given birth to when she was sixteen.

A few days later she told me that she'd decided to put a marker on the grave and wanted me to go to the monument company to choose a marker similar in size to the one marking the adjoining grave. She wanted the marker to have a lamb on it.

And she had decided on a name for the infant child. Dixie Lee. Dixie was Granny's name.

I said, "For you?" No, she said. Dixie Lee was the name of Bing Crosby's wife. She had always liked the name because she liked to listen to the smooth notes he sang.

A few weeks later I returned to Truett Cemetery, followed by a truck from the monument company. Near the cemetery gate, the man mixed a small batch of concrete in a wheelbarrow and pushed it across the tall grass to the grave. Because I was not sure on which side Dixie Lee was buried, my grandmother told me to choose one. I chose the north side, putting her that much closer to her mother.

For the past twenty summers I have returned to Truett Cemetery, to the grave of Dixie Lee, and have cleared the growth and smoothed the ground marking the site of Granny's never-forgotten child.

My grandmother, Dixie Moore, died only a few months after she found her daughter.

Published by permission of the author.

John Erickson, author of the popular *Hank the Cowdog* series of novels, has written several nonfiction books as well. This story is from his book *Friends: Cowboys, Cattle, Horses, Dogs, Cats, and 'Coons*. For more on the term "Cowboy Logic," listen to Michael Martin Murphey's song by that name.

# Clarence Herrington and Cowboy Logic

John Erickson

Clarence Herrington was a bachelor cowboy on the Lazy Y ranch and lived on the old Sam Handley place on Wolf Creek, about twenty miles south of Perryton, Texas.

Back in 1979 when I was cowboying for the Ellzey family, I used to drive past his house every day. You know how cowboys are; we notice the important things—the dogs, the grass in the horse pasture, what's in the back of a man's pickup, what's in the sick pen, how many staples are out of the fence.

Well, I began to notice that Clarence *always* had a bunch of clothes hanging on the clothesline behind his house.

That didn't make an impression on me at first, but after months of driving past his place and still seeing clothes hanging on the line, I started wondering about it.

Was it possible that he washed his clothes every day? No. That didn't fit what I knew of Clarence.

Day after day I puzzled over this mystery. Fall came, and then winter. The clothesline remained full, even on days when the temperature was down around zero.

Now, that wasn't right. Nobody, and especially a cowboy, would wash and hang out clothes in the dead of winter.

And then it hit me. Clarence had created a masterpiece of Cowboy Logic, right there in his back yard.

You see, a normal human being would wash clothes, hang them out to dry, gather them up in a basket, take them inside, iron them, fold them, and put them away in drawers.

Clarence had found a way of compressing all those steps down to three. He washed them, hung them on the line, and *left them there until he was ready to wear them.*

He let the wind do his ironing, he didn't need any folding, and he let the clothesline serve as a chest of drawers. Furthermore, all the noncowboys in the country thought that he was a real demon for cleanliness.

What a brilliant idea! The economy and simplicity of it almost brought tears to my eyes.

A couple of days later I met Clarence on the road. "I have just figured out why your clothesline is always full. Clarence, you have made me proud to be a cowboy!"

He grinned. "Makes you wonder how they can go on selling clothes dryers, don't it?"

From *Friends: Cowboys, Cattle, Horses, Dogs, Cats, and 'Coons* by John R. Erickson, Copyright 2002 John R. Erickson, reprinted by permission of the author and University of North Texas Press.

Red Steagall has been both the Cowboy Poet Laureate of Texas and the Poet Laureate of Texas as well as a popular western singer. "The Fence That Me and Shorty Built" is the title poem from a collection of some of his favorite verses. For more, see his website, redsteagall.com.

# The Fence That Me and Shorty Built

Red Steagall

We'd picked up all the fencing tools
And staples off the road.
An extra roll of 'bob' wire
Was the last thing left to load.

I drew a sleeve across my face
To wipe away the dirt.
The young man who was helping me
Was tuckin' in his shirt.

I turned around to him and said,
"This fence is finally done.

With five new strands of 'bob' wire
Shinin' proudly in the sun.

"The wire is runnin' straight and tight
With every post in line.
The kinda job you're proud of,
One that stands the test of time."

The kid was not impressed at all,
He stared off into space.
Reminded me of years ago,
Another time and place.

When I called myself a cowboy,
I was full of buck and bawl
I didn't think my hands would fit
Post augers and a maul.

But they sent me out with Shorty
And the ranch fence-building crew.
Well, I was quite insulted
And before the day was through,

I let him know that I'm a cowboy,
This ain't what I do.
I ain't no dadgummed nester,
I hired out to buckaroo.

He said, "We'll talk about that son,
When we get in tonight.
Right now you pick them augers up.
It's either that or fight."

Boy, I was diggin' post holes
Faster than a Georgia mole.
But if a rock got in my way
I simply moved the hole.

So when the cowboys set the posts,
The line went in and out.
Old Shorty's face got fiery red
And I can hear him shout.

"Nobody but a fool would build
A fence that isn't straight.
I got no use for someone who ain't
Pullin' his own weight."

Well, I thought for sure he'd hit me
Glad he didn't have a gun.
I looked around to find a place
Where I could duck and run.

But Shorty walked up to me
Just as calm as he could be.

Said, "Son, I need to talk to you,
Let's find ourselves a tree."

He rolled a Bull Durham cigarette
As we sat on the ground.
He took himself a puff or two
Then slowly looked around.

"Son, I ain't much on schoolin',
Didn't get too far with that.
But there's a lot of learnin'
Hidden underneath this hat.

"I got it all the hard way,
Every bump and bruise and fall.
Now some of it was easy,
But then most weren't fun a'tall.

"But one thing that I always got
From every job I've done,
Is do the best I can each day
And try to make it fun.

"I know that bustin' through them rocks
Ain't what you like to do.
By gettin' mad you've made it tough
On me and all the crew.

"Now you hired on to cowboy
And you think you've got the stuff.
You told him you're a good hand
And the boss has called your bluff.

"So how's that gonna make you look
When he comes ridin' through,
And he asks me who dug them holes
And I say it was you.

"Now we could let it go like this
And take the easy route.
But doin' things the easy way
Ain't what it's all about.

"The boss expects a job well done,
From every man he's hired.
He'll let you slide by once or twice,
Then one day you'll get fired.

"If you're not proud of what you do,
You won't amount to much.
You'll bounce around from job to job
Just slightly out of touch.

"Come mornin' let's re-dig those holes
And get that fence in line.

And you and I will save two jobs,
Those bein' yours and mine.

"And someday you'll come ridin' through
And look across this land,
And see a fence that's laid out straight
And know you had a hand,

"In something that's withstood the years.
Then proud and free from guilt,
You'll smile and say, 'Boys, that's the fence
That me and Shorty built.'"

Reprinted by permission of the author.

Tom Perini's cookbook, *Texas Cowboy Cooking*, came out more than fifteen years ago and continues to be one of the most popular cookbooks in Texas. Perini owns and operates Perini Ranch Steakhouse in Buffalo Gap and is in demand as a caterer. This stor.y is about an event he catered for legendary Albany rancher Watt Matthews.

# A Traditional Cowboy Dish

By Tom Perini

We did Watt Matthews's Princeton Class of '21 reunion party in 1989. There were only about twenty-five of them left in the class, but they were CEOs of big companies and all sorts of important people.

Watt wanted an authentic ranch party, so he asked us to fix a steer's head, which is a traditional cowboy dish, but I'd never done it. In fact, I'd never even seen it. The only reference I had was the movie *Giant*. In the movie, Elizabeth Taylor faints at the sight.

We knew it was roasted in the ground, so we just sort of figured it out. We left it in this underground oven for like eighteen hours. When it came time to pull this thing out of the ground, of course, I had all these old Princeton guys watching, and I had to play like this was an everyday event, and I'd never done it before in my life. So we got it out, unwrapped it and set it on the table.

And I remembered in the movie that they broke it open and served straight from the natural serving dish —and so did I, in front of this big audience. People came through the line and I served them up slices of meat and scoops of pit roasted brains, acting like I do this all the time.

Then this one lady came along and said, "I'm sorry, but I just can't eat that." And I said, "I understand." And she walked right by me and got a whole big plate of calf fries.

I just didn't have the heart to tell her.

*Editor's Note: Calf fries—or mountain oysters, as they are sometimes called—are a tasty West Texas dish consisting of fried calf testicles, rendered after castration. Tom Perini provides a recipe in his cookbook.*

From *Texas Cowboy Cooking* by Tom Perini, Copyright 2000, reprinted by permission of the author.

Joe W. Specht of Abilene is a Texas music historian and author with a special interest in West Texas and oil field music. This story is adapted from a longer article in the 2006 *West Texas Historical Association Yearbook*.

# Fiddlin' Friends: Bob Wills & Hoyle Nix

Joe W. Specht

On December 3, 1973, western swing and Texas music legend Bob Wills brought together a group of Texas Playboys alumni in the Sumet-Burnet Studio in Dallas, Texas, to record one more album, *For the Last Time*. At the personal invitation of Wills, Hoyle Nix and his twenty-one-year-old son Jody had driven in from Big Spring, Texas.

By 1973 Hoyle Nix and his band, the West Texas Cowboys, had been serving up western swing dance music—Bob Wills style—to the folks of the Permian

Basin, South Plains, and Concho Valley for more than twenty-five years. Nix and Wills were close friends, and Bob wanted Hoyle and Jody to be part of what became a very special event.

Bob Wills and Hoyle Nix first met in 1952. The West Texas Cowboys were the regular Friday night attraction at the American Legion Hall in Colorado City, Texas. And, as Hoyle tells the story, when Legion Hall officials learned that Wills and the Texas Playboys were making a swing through the region, they asked, "Would you move over for Bob Wills?" Nix replied, "More than happy to because I'd like to meet the man."

Later Nix had the opportunity to schedule the Texas Playboys to play The Stampede, the dance hall he and his younger brother Ben built outside of Big Spring on the Snyder highway.

Wills was born on a farm in Limestone County in 1905. When he was eight years old, the Wills family moved to Hall County near Memphis, Texas, to continue farming. Bob eventually took up residence in Turkey, the place he later referred to as "my hometown." Even though he departed the region in 1929, those years in West Texas stamped a lasting imprint on his music. Nix was born in 1918, in Azle, Texas. He arrived in West Texas the next year after his family moved to Big Spring, and Hoyle lived in and around Big Spring for the rest of his life.

In addition to similar farming backgrounds, the two men came from families with strong fiddling traditions. Wills learned his first fiddle tune at age nine; Nix was six years old when he played his first number. They were nurtured in the grand Texas frontier fiddle tradition of the long bow and the double stop, a tradition of breakdowns and waltzes. And they grew up with tunes like "Sally Goodin,'" "Billy in the Low Ground," "Crippled Turkey," "Sally Johnson," and "Great Big Taters in the Sandy Land" floating in the air.

Besides the common background—fiddlin' papas and the West Texas environment—another factor helped shape the relationship: Nix's unabashed admiration for Wills's music. Hoyle, almost thirteen years Bob's junior, had been a fan since the Light Crust Doughboys days of the early 1930s. As Hoyle recalled, "I thought [Wills] was the finest fiddle player that I ever heard."

When Nix formed the West Texas Cowboys in 1946 with brother Ben, they patterned the band after the Texas Playboys.

Further proof of Nix's regard for Wills is evidenced by the names he chose for two of his children. Youngest son Jody was born in 1952, the same year Bob and Hoyle met. Hoyle named Jody after long-time Texas Playboy and left-handed fiddler Joe Holley because he thought his son might be left-handed, too, and he was. Nix called his youngest daughter Robin, after Robert in James Robert Wills, because she was born on March 6, Bob's birthday.

However, Hoyle Nix was no mere Bob Wills imitator. Nix openly acknowledged his primary musical influence: "Just Mr. Wills." But as Texas music historian Kevin Coffey correctly points out, Nix had his own sound, a sound "in many ways different from Wills," a sound "true to his arid West Texas—dryer, less overtly jazzy and leaning more toward honky-tonk than most western swing bands."

When Wills's and Nix's paths crossed in Colorado City in 1952, the West Texas Cowboys were fast becoming the go-to band in the area. Nix already had a regional hit, "Big Ball's in Cowtown." But he remained a maverick, content to stay put in Big Spring, recording when it was convenient for small Texas record companies and performing within a 150-mile radius of Big Spring to enthusiastic, loyal crowds an average of four nights a week. Nix and his West Texas Cowboys could hold their own with any band—even the Texas Playboys.

With a budding friendship in the works and mutual respect all around, Bob and Hoyle struck on the idea to book their two bands together at some of the same dances when Wills rolled through the area. And for the next twelve years—three to four times a year—the Texas Playboys and the West Texas Cowboys shared the stage in a battle of the bands format. In addition to larger towns such as Abilene, Midland, and Big Spring at The Stampede, these encounters also took place in the likes of Brownfield, Slaton, and Sweetwater. On occasion, Wills invited Nix up on the bandstand to perform a fiddle number with the Texas Playboys, which Hoyle called a dream come true.

The battle dances also gave the Texas Playboys an opportunity to better get to know the Nix brothers, and in the late 1950s a contingent of the Wills band made the move to Big Spring to sign on with the West Texas Cowboys. Guitarist and arranger Eldon Shamblin was the first to arrive in 1957. The next year fiddler/saxophonist Louis "Louie" Tierney and piano pounder Millard Kelso made the switch; then fiddler Henry Boatman and pianist Mancel Tierney followed. These former Texas Playboys stayed in various combinations through the early 1960s, and during this period, the West Texas Cowboys grew to its largest size with ten members.

How did Shamblin, Tierney, and the rest end up with Nix? "Well, they went to work for me," Hoyle explains. "Nothing against their boss man, Bob. They just kind of got tired of the road, you know. He traveled so much, and they kind of wanted to just stop and rest for a while."

Don Walser, who made a name for himself in Austin in the 1990s as "the Pavarotti of the Plains," offers a humorous aside: "When they wanted to quit drinking, they would go to Hoyle. He was kinda the Betty Ford of West Texas; he wouldn't let 'em drink and he'd work 'em out there on the farm and he'd sweat some of that stuff out of 'em."

That brings up the subject of alcohol. The Wills-Nix relationship is perhaps even more unique because of Wills's drinking habits and Nix's non-indulgence. Bob's bouts with the bottle, which adversely affected both his career and personal life, are legendary. On the other hand, Hoyle was a teetotaler who expected anyone in his band to practice abstinence, too (son Jody continues to apply the same rule even today). Steel guitarist Bill Schlotter wryly recollected, "Hoyle was so strict. If Hoyle had had Bob Wills himself in the band drinking, he'd even fired him."

After his second heart attack in 1964, Wills relinquished final control of the Texas Playboys. Without a band, Bob took on solo engagements, bringing along his own vocalist, first Joe Andrews and later Tagg Lambert. And Wills continued to meet up with Nix—now with the billing "Bob Wills and Hoyle Nix and his West Texas Cowboys"—until a series of strokes forced him off the road for good in 1969. Wills also had occasion to offer a tip of the hat to Nix in the recording studio. In a 1966 session for Kapp Records, Bob waxed a version of "Big Ball's in Cowtown."

In April 1973, Wills returned to Turkey, Texas, for the unveiling of a granite monument erected in his honor.

Nix appeared as well to play the evening dance, and the West Texas Cowboys became a regular attraction in the ensuing years for the annual Bob Wills Day celebration held in Turkey on the last Saturday in April.

In September, Wills came back to The Stampede for one of his last public appearances. Wheelchair-bound and unable to fiddle, Wills sang only one song. He turned to Nix and instructed, "Hoyle, kick 'Sittin' on Top of the World' off in G."

After the dance, Bob told Hoyle if there should be an opportunity to record again he wanted Nix to be there. And three months later Hoyle and Jody joined Wills in the Sumet-Burnet Studio in Dallas along with the Texas Playboys.

The *For the Last Time* sessions were planned for two days, and the Nix presence is in evidence almost from the beginning. At Wills's request, Hoyle's fiddle is featured on "Comin' Down from Denver" and the traditional "Crippled Turkey." Nix takes the lead vocal on two numbers, including "Big Ball's in Cowtown," plus he contributes his share of the "ah ha"s. Wills also thought highly of Jody's vocal stylings, and one of the three songs he wanted the younger Nix to sing was the Cindy Walker-penned "When You Leave Amarillo." In fact, Bob's interjection—"Cut out the lights!"—at the conclusion of the song is the last he ever made on record.

Confined in a wheelchair, Wills soon tired, however, and after six songs, he returned home to rest. During the night Bob suffered what was most likely another stroke, from which he never recovered. The next day, without Wills on hand, the mood was somber, but recording continued with Hoyle again providing the Wills-like ad libs. Charles R. Townsend, Wills's biographer who attended the sessions, reported that when the band recorded "San Antonio Rose" and "Hoyle Nix took Bob's part and hollered, there were few dry eyes in the entire studio, because Hoyle sounded so much like Bob."

Bob Wills died on May 13, 1975. Hoyle, Ben, and Jody, along with West Texas Cowboys' guitarist Don Tolle, drove from Big Spring to attend the funeral in Tulsa. Two years later Nix returned to the Sumet-Burnet Studio to make what turned out to be his final recordings. Hoyle included some Wills selections—"San Antonio Rose" and "Lilly Dale"—along with a batch of old-time fiddle tunes—"Gray Eagle," "Billy in the Low Ground," and "Hopping Lucy."

The liner notes for the album, *Hoyle Nix & His West Texas Cowboys Texas Style,* proudly state, "Hoyle has worked with the great Bob Wills, his closest friend since 1952."

Published by permission of the author, condensed from *"Great Big Taters in the Sandy Land: The Musical Friendship of Bob Wills & Hoyle Nix," 2006 West Texas Historical Association Yearbook.*

Tumbleweed Smith is a popular radio celebrity, newspaper columnist, speaker, and entertainer, based in Big Spring.

# Classical Piano in the Oil Patch

Tumbleweed Smith

Ann Houser taught private piano lessons in Big Spring. She was a tyrant. She thought all of her students would one day become concert pianists and be popular the world over. She was well known throughout the state. When Ferrante and Teicher, the famous piano duo, came to Big Spring for a concert, they ended up at Ann's house and played until the wee hours for a few invited guests.

My wife Susan took lessons from Ann. "I was not her best student," says Susan. "She and my mom were friends and they both expected more from me. I felt I was under pressure all the time to play better. Once at a recital I got to play a duet with a friend of mine who was an exceptional piano player. Ann Houser complimented me on my playing. It was such a special moment I'll always remember it. Once when my parents were out of town I spent the night at Ann's house and learned she was a real human being, not just a demanding teacher."

Ann's daughter, Susan Houser Brinegar, is a musician and has made appearances in Europe. She is also an artist whose paintings are on display in homes, galleries, and museums around the country. Susan lives in Phoenix now and enjoys telling stories about her mother, who at one time lived in a tent in the oil patch near Forsan.

"My dad wanted her to have a little more upbeat life than just sitting in a tent. So he put a wooden floor in the tent and had glass beads hanging down to separate the rooms. He bought cheap Persian-like rugs to put down and he bought her a piano. So she spent her days and evenings playing the piano. Dad would sometimes work the night shift. So she would play all night and then fix breakfast for him the next morning and they would go to sleep.

"Once while Dad was working, Mom was playing some Chopin at about two or three o'clock in the morning. She heard a car drive up and she wondered why is Ed, my father, getting home early from the oil field. So she went to the door and walking up was this man. His wife was sitting in the car.

"He told my mom, 'We are totally lost. We're in the middle of an oil field and we don't know how to get out of it. And I could not believe it when I heard Chopin's music coming from a tent in the middle of an oil field. Was that you?'

"My mom replied that it was indeed she who was playing the piano. The man commented on how beautiful it was. My mom thanked him and told the man, 'My husband will help you out of the oil field but he won't be home until morning. Would you like to come in?'

"So they went inside, she fixed them coffee and she played for them the rest of the night. When morning came, she fixed breakfast for them when Dad came home and they left, saying they would always remember Texas because of hearing Chopin in an oil field."

Published by permission of the author.

Bobby Weaver spins a lot of good yarns in his book, *Hotter'n Pecos and Other West Texas Lies*, including this story from the oil patch.

# Graduation Night

Bobby D. Weaver

Graduation night in Wink was always a big deal. All the seniors, decked out in mortarboards and long black robes, paraded one by one up on the auditorium stage to receive their diplomas. The whole town turned out for the event. Afterwards there was a dance at the gym and later on a midnight supper, served this particular year at the First Baptist Church. Some graduates slipped off after the dance in favor of one of the local honky-tonks to experience earthier pleasures. But Bill took no part in any of the festivities beyond receiving his diploma.

By 11 P.M. he was sitting on the front stoop of his folks' house with a sack lunch in his clenched right hand.

Beside him, rolled in a neat bundle, was a new pair of overalls, a clean work shirt, a pair of steel-toed Red Wing work boots, and two pairs of canvas Boss Walloper work gloves. He was waiting for the crew car to arrive and take him out to Consolidated's Rig #4 where he would be working backup tongs as a roughneck.

Like a lot of kids born and reared in the oil patch, Bill considered a good-paying roughnecking job the pinnacle of success. By the time the graveyard crew picked him up, he was about as excited as any eighteen-year-old could get, except for maybe that time he scored the winning touchdown again Pyote in district playoffs. At last, he was getting somewhere in life. He was going to be a man and have bragging rights in the local beer joints, just like all the other oil-field hands he knew.

After relieving the evening tour crew, the driller sent Bill and the lead tong man down into the cellar to finish installing the blowout preventer. The tong man, of course, had already been ribbing Bill pretty hard about finishing high school. As they made their way down beneath the rig floor, he started in again. This time he questioned the intelligence of any high school graduate who went around with a pair of Boss Wallopers stuffed in his hip pocket.

It took about thirty minutes to get everything arranged so they could lower the heavy blowout preventer into place. Bill was brushing some dirt off the base flange when it happened. They never did figure out just what caused it, but at that very moment the preventer fell with a crash. Bill managed to jerk his hands partially back before the massive hunk of iron smashed the ends of his Boss Wallopers flat as a pancake. The kid just stood there for what seemed an eternity, his face losing color as red began to stain the fingers of both gloves. Finally, he eased his hands out of the gloves and fearfully inspected all ten of his digits. Incredibly, they were all there except for the tips of both middle fingers, which were slightly nipped. That was the last time the crew saw Bill.

Four years later, almost to the day, graduation night rolled around again. Once again Bill participated, this time receiving his hard-won diploma on a college campus. Beneath his graduation robe, however, firmly tucked in his hip pocket, was a pair of fingerless Boss Wallopers—a reminder of what he had missed by leaving the patch.

From *Hotter 'n Pecos and Other West Texas Lies*, by Bobby D. Weaver, Copyright © 2010 by Bobby D. Weaver. Reprinted with the permission of The Permissions Company, Inc., on behalf of Texas Tech University Press (ttupress.org).

Andy Wilkinson of Lubbock, who penned this ballad in 1989, is a songwriter, singer, poet, and playwright. Through his poems and songs, he weaves images of people and places in telling the tales of the American West of yesterday and today.

# The Tumbleweed Christmas Tree

Andy Wilkinson

It was a rough year for a roughneck's children,
Hard times, and harder livin';
We moved when the rent come due, and it come due
once a week.
That year, in late December,
Found us in an old house trailer,
West of Odessa, near a town they call Notrees.

Too poor to pay attention,
Daddy lived on good intentions,
And he intended Christmas to be just what we believed.
Drove to town in the company pickup,

But when he didn't have the sawbuck
For the price of a Christmas tree, he brought back
    a tumbleweed.

CHORUS:

    Christmas Eve in Notrees, Texas,
    Wind blowin' through the cactus,
    Santa Claus was a rich kid's saint and a poor
    kid's dream.
    But I'd trade every fancy present
    I ever had, or ever will get
    For the night of the tumbleweed Christmas tree.

Daddy set it on the dinette table,
Momma made a newsprint angel,
Ornaments of tin-foil scraps, buttons on a string.
It took us all night to decorate it;
When we got done, I'll have to say that
It was the prettiest tumbleweed I'd ever seen.

Wind rocked the trailer like a cradle,
While we sang our Christmas carols,
Sittin' on the sofa on the duct-taped Naugahyde.
Daddy looked proud as a big-city banker,
Momma tried hard to be thankful,
But lookin' at the tumbleweed, she laughed until
    she cried.

CHORUS:

Christmas Eve in Notrees, Texas,
Wind blowin' through the cactus,
Santa Claus was a rich kid's saint and a poor
kid's dream.
But I'd trade every fancy present
I ever had, or ever will get
For the night of the tumbleweed Christmas tree.

Now, I was just six, goin' on seven,
But bein' poor is an education,
And that night I learned a lot about just what
Christmas means:
It means love, and it means lovin',
It means money don't mean nothin',
And it means a tumbleweed can make a Christmas tree.

CHORUS:

Christmas Eve in Notrees, Texas,
Wind blowin' through the cactus,
Santa Claus was a rich kid's saint and a poor
kid's dream.
But I'd trade every fancy present
I ever had, or ever will get
For the night of the tumbleweed Christmas tree.

Reprinted by permission of the author, © 1989, D. A. Wilkinson, (Cain't Quit Music, BMI).

Jim Richmond grew up in Midland and is now a bank president in Abilene. He wrote this prize-winning guest column in 1994, published in the *Abilene Reporter-News*.

# Suzanne Wasn't the Problem

Jim Richmond

Suzanne was not the prettiest girl in Mrs. Short's second grade class at Sam Houston Elementary School in Midland in 1963. She was probably the best dressed but was clumsy in her actions. She talked when she should be listening and her words were not clear. She looked older than the rest of us but acted younger.

Because we all knew she was different, she became the target of our childish but cruel remarks. Suzanne didn't seem to know she was different, and when she was teased she just smiled and said, "Fank you." She had difficulty making the "th" sound, among other speech impediments.

I had never known anyone like her, and I regret that I never got to know her. Suzanne had Down syndrome.

On an afternoon only about three weeks into the school year, I looked out the window to see if the clouds had cleared enough to allow me to play with my friends after class. I was impressed with the long white Cadillac I saw pull up in front of the school. I was sure that it had to belong to a movie star.

The woman I saw emerge from the driver's side, a woman that would have a lasting effect on my life, was dressed as if she had stepped off an MGM set. I was stunned to see she was making her way to my classroom. I remember that she had the blondest hair I had ever seen, the darkest sunglasses and what seemed to be very heavy feet. Each step seemed an effort as she approached the door to the classroom.

I was sitting at the back of the class next to Suzanne when this woman knocked on the door. When Mrs. Short opened the door I heard the quivering voice of the blonde say, "I've come for Suzanne. I'm taking her home."

"No fair!" I heard one of my friends say. "It isn't time to go home. How come she gets to go early?"

As Suzanne's mother entered the classroom she removed her sunglasses to reveal eyes swollen from tears. As she approached her daughter's desk, I remember those eyes. I think it was the first time I realized that not everyone had brown eyes. I had never seen an adult cry before and I knew something terrible must have happened.

I felt hypnotized as this woman approached, her eyes glaring through me yet spouting tears with each step she took. It was the first time I ever saw a person with a broken heart.

"I stay here," Suzanne said, "with my friends."

"No, we're going home," said her mother. "They are not your friends."

It had never occurred to me that she thought of us as her friends. No one was very nice to her or even acted like she belonged in our class. To Suzanne, we were still friends of hers.

That night I lay in bed thinking of Suzanne, her mother and the events of the day. Suzanne's mother was obviously very affluent, even for a 1960s Midlander. Her life seemed so perfect to me except for her daughter.

As I lay there, I thought of Suzanne's mother's sadness and then I began to think of her eyes and how it looked to see an adult cry.

Then the realization hit my eight-year-old mind like a tornado. It wasn't Suzanne that was the problem. That wasn't what made her cry. Suzanne was happy and liked everyone. It was my imperfections and those of my classmates, not Suzanne's, that had upset her mother. I had been a part of something terribly wrong.

No, I had never taken part in making fun of Suzanne, but I had done worse. I had done nothing. I had never defended her. It was my actions and those of my classmates that had broken the heart of someone I didn't even know.

The next morning I practically ran to school. I was going to make it up to Suzanne and her mother. I was going to see to it that Suzanne felt like a part of our class. I was a leader in the class. I could influence the other kids to be nice to her. She was going to be sitting by me at lunch every day if that is what she wanted.

When I got to school that day, Suzanne wasn't at her desk. "Maybe she is just late," I thought. Suzanne wasn't just late. She didn't come back to school again. Her mother had taken her out of our school to avoid the unkindness she was experiencing from her classmates. She wasn't just leaving early the day before. She was leaving for good.

That realization haunted me for several years. I had failed miserably in my responsibilities. I was sure that whenever I was made fun of, it was my payback for not defending Suzanne.

Two years later I was at the movies and saw Suzanne sitting on a bench. Several older kids were kidding her unmercifully and laughing at her, and she sat there smiling. "Fank you," she said. I knew this was my chance to redeem myself.

"Give her a break, guys," I said. "Leave her alone."

As I walked away, I didn't feel the lift I thought I would when I approached the situation. I really didn't know those kids, so I had nothing to risk. They weren't really my peers. I had salvaged nothing. I had only done what anyone would do.

I never saw Suzanne again. Not in person, anyway. I did see her smiling face every time I saw someone being bullied. I would also see her mother's eyes reflecting her broken heart when I felt I didn't have the strength to stand up to some bully.

Now, when my son Kris leaves for school, I often wonder if it is as hard to be a kid as it was when I was in school. I pray that today's young people are kinder than we were.

You see, Kris isn't really the best-looking kid in his sixth-grade class at Madison Middle School. He dresses nice enough, but he is clumsy and talks when he should listen. Kris is older than he acts, but he smiles a beautiful smile. Before he leaves me he always says, "I wuv you, Daddy." Kris has trouble with "L" sounds and other parts of his speech. You see, my Kris, like Suzanne, also has Down syndrome.

Reprinted by permission of the author and the *Abilene Reporter-News.*

George Dolan wrote a front page humor column, This Is West Texas, for the *Fort Worth Star-Telegram* for thirty years. The following story is from a collection, *Dolan: The Best & The Rest*, published in 1989, the year after Dolan died.

# A Trip Cut Short

George Dolan

A rancher from far West Texas told a cattle buyer, as the rancher's cattle were being rounded up for sale, that as soon as it was done he was taking his wife on a trip up into the Pacific Northwest. The rancher had bought a fancy camping van, with all the accessories.

A couple of months later the buyer was back in that area. He dropped by to see the rancher. "How was your trip to the Northwest?" the buyer asked.

The rancher's eyes hardened. His face reddened. His wife snickered. "I might as well tell you," the rancher said, sighing heavily. "If I don't, she will."

The morning that the last steer was loaded, the rancher said, he went back home. His wife had their new vehicle all packed. They started out immediately. Early in the afternoon, the rancher's wife said, "You're all tired out. Why don't you climb in the back and take a nap while I drive?"

He saw no flaw in that suggestion. He got into the back, stripped down to his shorts, and crawled into a bunk. He slept until nearly dark.

When he awakened, the vehicle was stopped. He crawled out of the bunk, opened the back door a crack, and peered out. He was in a small town. His wife had stopped at a traffic light. Just then, the light changed. The vehicle lurched forward. The rancher pitched out the back.

There he was, in downtown somewhere, in his undershorts. He began running after his wife, yelling. She didn't hear him.

You can't run around nearly nude in downtown anywhere without attracting attention. In no time at all, two officers in a patrol car drew alongside him. He explained his situation. They told him to get in and sped after his wife.

They soon caught up with her. They turned on red blinking lights and siren. As she was rolling to a stop, the patrol car drew alongside. She looked over, saw a near-naked husband—who was supposed to be sleeping in the back—and did what any normal woman would do. She fainted.

The camping van jumped a curb and rolled to a stop against a telephone pole. The officers revived the rancher's wife while the rancher was hurriedly getting dressed. Order was restored and all hands had a good laugh.

Then the rancher insisted on buying dinner for the officers. After a meal in a nearby restaurant, the rancher picked up the check and got to his feet. His wife tugged on his sleeve and whispered to him. He hadn't finished dressing.

He sat back down and furtively zipped a zipper. Then he stood again and started toward the cashier's stand. When he walked away, the tablecloth was jerked off the table. Dishes and silverware crashed to the floor. The tablecloth had gotten caught in his zipper.

The man, flushed, sat down and tugged at the zipper. Finally, he took out his pocket knife, stood, whacked off a piece of the tablecloth, walked over to the cashier, and said: "Tell me what I owe you for the dinner—and everything."

He paid, helped his wife into the camping van, turned around, drove back home and, the next day, took the vehicle back to the dealer and said, "Sell it for whatever you can get."

Reprinted by permission of the *Fort Worth Star Telegram*.

After reading a newspaper article about iconic Texas Ranger Joaquin Jackson in 1986, an El Paso Methodist minister, Charles R. Graff, wrote a letter to the Texas Ranger Hall of Fame about an encounter with Jackson many years earlier when both were in South Texas. Jackson retired from the Rangers in 1993 and passed away in 2016. He wrote two books about his Ranger years—*One Ranger* and *One Ranger Returns.* The letter from Graff ran as an appendix in the first book.

# Joaquin Jackson at Work

Charles R. Graff

In 1968, I was a young lawyer just a year or two out of law school practicing law in Brownsville, Texas. Our law firm was doing a great deal of criminal law practice and as a young fellow those were exciting times. Our job was made far easier by the slipshod investigative techniques of many of the area peace officers.

These were the years just following the Miranda decision and it seems that peace officers, or at least those we dealt with, had yet to figure out how to investigate and gather evidence within the framework of the U.S. Constitution. The law enforcement community groaned loudly under the burden of Miranda and it was said by some that there was no way you could get a confession under those restrictions.

There was a series of thefts of mercury from gas well meters in Cameron County. Mercury was commanding a high price and there was a real problem with these thefts. The local authorities were unable to catch the culprits and the Rangers were asked to assist in the investigation. The Rangers were successful and two brothers were arrested. The brothers had a Harley Davidson motorcycle and used this to get around in the country to commit their crime and make their escape. Our law firm was retained to represent the brothers.

I was drinking coffee at the stand-up bar in the rotunda of the old Cameron County Courthouse when Ranger Joaquin Jackson walked up to me and spoke. He asked if I was one of the lawyers representing the brothers. I said yes I was. He told me it was his intention to go over to the jail at 1 P.M. and question the brothers. He said he wanted me to know so I could be present if I wished to confer with my clients on this matter. He was businesslike but very polite.

This was a first for me! Never before and never since had a peace officer informed me of his upcoming interrogation. They usually tried to play a cat-and-mouse game with the defense attorneys, so this straightforward approach was something new. I was impressed but thought to myself that Jackson had just cooked his own goose. The brothers were professional criminals and were at least a match for Jackson.

I had something else to do at one o'clock and did not perceive Jackson's activity to be much of a threat. But as a safeguard, I went by the jail and spoke with the brothers. I told them that after lunch this big tall fellow named Joaquin Jackson was going to come over and try to interrogate them. I added that he was a Texas Ranger and his only purpose was to put them in prison. Both of them had previously served time in prison, and they knew what prison was all about.

I told them to say nothing, not even to tell their names or respond to questions. "Just sit and look at him; don't even speak to him," I said. I then reminded them that they had been through this kind of thing before and asked if they thought they needed me there to help them keep their mouths shut. Their response was that they knew the ropes and certainly didn't need any help to resist the questions of a peace officer. Confident that Jackson could do no harm, I went my way.

About midafternoon, the secretary came in and told me that Ranger Jackson was in the office and wanted to see me. She ushered him in and he placed his briefcase on my desk and opened it. He handed me the carbon copies of the signed confessions of the brothers. He once again in a very businesslike manner told me that I was entitled to have copies of these confessions. With that and a short goodbye he left. I have never seen him since.

I was stunned! I was shocked! How could this happen? Convinced that he could not have obtained these confessions without violating the rights of the brothers, I rushed over to the jail so I could photograph their bruises and begin to try and break their confessions.

When I got there, there were no bruises or marks on the brothers. I began to question them, looking for a violation of their rights or anything I could use to have their confessions thrown out.

"Did he beat you?" I asked. "No," they replied.

"Did he threaten you?" I asked. "No," they replied.

"Did he promise you a lighter sentence or try to make a deal with you," I asked. "No," they replied.

"Then why, why did you sign that confession? Why did you even talk to him?"

They looked down at the floor and finally one of them looked at me with a tear in his eye and said, "He is the nicest man I ever met."

The conversation disclosed that he had told them that it was about time for them to get their lives straightened out and this was their last chance. I don't know how it worked out for them, but at that time, in that place, that is what they intended to do.

I have always considered that the finest piece of police work that I have ever seen. Intelligence, sensitivity, creativity, and a knowledge of the human animal accomplished what bluster and brute force never could have accomplished. Those that say they can't be effective peace officers within the framework of the U.S. Constitution have never seen Joaquin Jackson at work. He is a first-rate role model for what modern peace officers should be.

In 1970, I left the practice of law and became a Methodist preacher. I still from time to time reflect on that part of my life, and one of the bright spots was seeing Joaquin Jackson practice his profession. May his tribe increase!

Reprinted by permission of the Texas Ranger Hall of Fame.

After a devastating tornado ripped through Wichita Falls on April 10, 1979, *Fort Worth Star-Telegram* special assignments writer Jerry Flemmons filed this account.

# Wichita Falls: A City under Siege

Jerry Flemmons

The first hook left the black shelf of clouds as a swirling spike of dark wind.

"Evil-looking thing," said an awed onlooker.

That was ten miles southwest of the city beyond the beige waters of Lake Wichita and the Astroturf of Memorial Stadium.

The warning siren blew at 5:20 P.M., herald to that genesis of a tornado.

Long minutes passed.

The second hook—a funnel that does not touch the ground—dropped, swinging clumsily as a broken pendulum, the witness said, then was sucked again into the sky.

Now the hook was nearer, five miles from the football stadium.

The second siren came at 5:45 P.M.

A third hook appeared moments later, and a fourth.

Then a funnel touched down three miles from the stadium.

At 5:50 P.M. the siren blew for the last time.

"And blew, and blew, and blew, and blew," recalled a survivor.

And then it stopped, she said, and she heard the sound.

High above the stadium, a pair of hooks mated and birthed a tornado.

Almost casually, it slapped at the stadium press box and crumpled the steel house into the stands.

It rose, skipping high, and settled again, toppling twelve-inch-thick light standards rimming a baseball field, leaving them drooping like dead broken sunflowers.

The tornado moved east, slightly north, slanting across heavily populated and mostly expensive housing areas of Wichita Falls: Lakeview Manor, Meadowlake, Western Hills, Faith Village, Colonial Park, and Southmoor.

"It was a black cloud, dancing along on two tails," said a witness, Joey Snyder, hypnotized by the swirling drama of the skies.

Two thousand feet wide, it moved with agonizingly slow and methodical precision for fourteen to fifteen minutes.

It simply demolished everything in its path, the most expensive and destructive tornado in Texas history. Entire blocks of homes disappeared. Two thousand homes are estimated to have been destroyed. A shopping mall fell. Businesses large and small. McNeil Junior High, empty at that late hour, was stripped of bricks and whipped by the wind's tail.

Forty-two are dead. More than a thousand more are injured, some of whom surely will die. At least 500 emergency operations were performed at city hospitals.

"I wouldn't be surprised if we had a hundred dead in the final count," said Mayor Kenneth Hill.

Wichita Falls is a dazed, stunned, crippled city.

Lying in the vortex of the ominous-sounding Tornado Alley of North Texas and Southern Oklahoma, the Black Tuesday of Wichita Falls began as day was ending.

The almost total devastation inside the one-half-mile-wide, eight-mile-long corridor was terrible enough, but the aftermath left it as a city under siege by disaster.

The tornado broke the city's main power cable. Telephone lines were blown away. Water and gas lines were cut off in much of the city.

That was the night.

"We just lay there all night," said a woman. "We slept in sleeping bags on the living room floor. We had no roof. The walls were gone. We just lay there and waited. I cried."

Without electricity, Wichita Falls's civil defense plan was severely crippled. In a practice alert two weeks ago, it was perfect. Without electricity and phones and water, however, the plan faltered.

At first a thousand volunteers moved throughout the town, laboring under a full moon glazed over by a dusty sky, searching for survivors.

By dawn, thousands of other volunteers began arriving, some from as far away as Fort Worth and Dallas and Lubbock. Perhaps there were as many as ten thousand volunteers, including airmen from Sheppard Air Force Base and Fort Sill in Oklahoma, National Guard units, Boy Scouts, police civilian reserve teams, and just plain people who came to help the troubled city.

At sunset of the second day, Wednesday, the Wichita Falls City Council passed an emergency ordinance declaring what everyone knew, that the city was in a state of disaster.

Gov. Bill Clements had come and seen it. Sen. John Tower had returned to his hometown, toured the disaster area by helicopter and said of it—"I don't recall ever having seen any natural disaster of this proportion, and I've seen lots of them."

Both Clements and Tower promised to have Wichita Falls declared a national disaster area.

The city council additionally put the city under a 9:00 P.M. curfew, and installed strict police patrols to forestall looting and vandalism.

The council also ordered that retail prices could not be raised on essential items such as food, ice, toilet paper, construction equipment, matches, motel and hotel rentals, and restaurant meals.

Fines were to be up to $200 for offenses.

None of that mattered. Gas already was selling as high as $1.50 a gallon at several of the few stations which remained open. One man was selling flashlight batteries for $1.00 each.

Throughout the city, food and other essentials disappeared from grocery shelves. Candles were impossible to find. Long lines queued at convenience stores buying beer and soft drinks before they became hot in the now-dead refrigerators. Melting ice cream was selling for half price.

And all day Wednesday, a wind gusting up to forty-five miles per hour thrashed workers as they searched through rubble for more and more victims.

All of this happened under a sky thick with West Texas dust, leaving an eerie yellow shadow sheen on the tornado's trail of tears.

People were gathering together what was left, loading the debris of living onto trailers and into pickups throughout the day, some leaving to stay with friends, others to settle into emergency housing established in churches and the Salvation Army headquarters.

"You have to kind of laugh," said one. "It's so tragic. Everything's gone. People are dead, and all I have left is my cookie jar."

Inside the jar, the sugar cookies were unbroken.

All over Wichita Falls there were dramas.

Inside the entrance of Wichita General Hospital, where most victims were taken, Hazel Bryant wandered the halls.

"I can't find my daughter," she said.

Her daughter and son-in-law's home was destroyed. She has not heard of them nor seen them since.

The hospital was serviced by huge water tanks ferried in from Fort Sill. The military base also furnished an auxiliary generator to augment the hospital's already-overloaded backup unit.

Traffic around the hospital and at the two funeral homes where the dead victims were taken was backed up for several blocks in all directions.

The eight-mile path of destruction was encircled by curious sightseers, which hampered the movements of emergency vehicles and also the residents trying to salvage and remove their few remaining personal goods.

Inside that path of the tornado were all the clichés associated with twisters—pieces of glass driven through tree trunks, telephone poles broken in half, cars flipped. The excrement of the tornado littered the countryside.

Mesquite trees were stripped of leaves. In their place, the tornado left behind pieces of housing insulation which hung like Christmas tree angel hair in the bare branches.

The capricious tornado moved with a pattern of systematic deadliness. Here it decimated an entire block. There it skipped every other house in the block, destroying one house and hardly riffling roof tiles in the next.

Where it struck, however, the results often were amazing. A liquor store with roof blown away and two walls removed and liquor bottles still sitting unbroken on shelves. Closets, all rooms around them destroyed, yet with clothes still hanging inside. Curtains blowing gently through windows of a room with only one wall remaining.

The tornado moved through several districts of expensive homes, many in the $200,000 range. One, a massive multistory glass, brick, and wood modern structure, was reduced to a $200,000 pile of rubble with nothing substantial left standing.

The owner climbed to the top of his expensive rubble and erected an American flag.

Then he walked away, simply walked away, from what once was his home.

*Editor's Note: Despite the prediction of more deaths, the death toll remained at forty-two. More than seventeen hundred were injured, more than three thousand homes were destroyed, and twenty thousand were left homeless for a time, according to the National Weather Service.*

Reprinted by permission, *Fort Worth Star-Telegram.*

Charlena Chandler of Midland, a longtime teacher in Iraan, writes in her book *Shakespeare on the Pecos* about a joyful moment she and West Texans everywhere would always remember. It took place at a high school football game in Marfa on a Friday night, October 16, 1987.

# A Most Joyful Moment

Charlena Chandler

On a cool, perfect football kind of evening in Marfa, back when it was just a small town known for cattle ranching and the legacy of *Giant,* way before the days of Prada and the trendy crowd, both sides of the high school stadium were packed. Just before kickoff, the Marfa Shorthorns and the Iraan Braves champed at the bit, standing on their respective sidelines with adrenalin pumping.

The game's play-by-play commentator paused in his pre-game routine . . . nothing but silence from the press box. Then the announcement:

"The baby's out of the well!"

The elation that followed united the crowd of fans and players on both sides. The ensuing roar was deafening. On the field, the players slapped teammates' shoulders, as if they had won the Super Bowl. Coaches pumped fists. From my vantage point on the fifty-yard line, it was an electrifying moment because we, to a person, understood the announcement:

"The baby's out of the well!"

As a junior in high school, my son was a Brave on the field. A fellow teacher, Mrs. Settle, had accompanied my dad and me as we made the long drive to Marfa, and we had listened to the radio the entire way, as the saga of Baby Jessica was played out. By the time we reached our destination, we knew rescue was near, but so many things could have gone wrong. Would the baby survive?

It had been a vigil of fifty-eight hours.

On October 14, an eighteen-month-old baby girl, Jessica McClure, had fallen into an eight-inch pipe (from an abandoned well) in her backyard in Midland.

An incredible effort, with new technology and superhuman endurance, ensued. The nation watched. And now the happy ending.

Baby Jessica, as she was called, is a grown woman today, a wife and mother. She does not recall her ordeal.

But those of us who were waiting in Marfa will always remember, not who won the game on that Friday night, but the joy of hearing—

"The baby's out of the well!"

*Editor's Note: Jessica's story was made into a television movie in 1989,* Everybody's Baby: The Rescue of Jessica McClure, *starring Patty Duke and Beau Bridges. Odessa American photographer Scott Shaw won the 1988 Pulitzer Prize for Spot News Photography for his photograph of the rescue.*

From *Shakespeare on the Pecos* by Charlena Chandler, reprinted by permission of the author.

After observing an adult literacy class in 1991, *Abilene Reporter-News* editor Glenn Dromgoole wrote this piece about semicolons.

# Any Semicolons around Here?

Glenn Dromgoole

It's not often that one gets involved in a good philosophical discussion about semicolons. I happened to observe one. It was what is known in education as "the teachable moment."

Several members of the Taylor County Adult Literacy Council were visiting a literacy class. The teacher, Judy Berry, was working with six adults who are learning to read and write.

She had the students take turns reading sentences from a beginning textbook. Most of the sentences were short and simple. She urged them to plow ahead through the book so they could get on to more difficult and interesting material.

Then one of the students asked a question. He pointed to something in the textbook and asked Mrs. Berry what it was.

"That's a semicolon," she replied. What happened next was pure art—the art of teaching.

She asked if anyone knew what a semicolon was. No one did. She walked to the chalkboard and wrote a sentence: "I am looking for her; I have money for her." She told the students that a semicolon is used to join two very short sentences.

"What else might we have used to join these sentences?" she asked. "We might have said, 'I am looking for her because I have money for her.' Or 'I am looking for her, and I have money for her.'"

The students joined in the discussion. One said she had never seen a semicolon in the letters she receives. Another thought maybe she had seen one in a letter from school sent home to parents. That sent Mrs. Berry back to the chalkboard to write a sentence that might be sent home from school: "We were going to have a meeting; however, it was canceled."

Another student, probably in his early fifties, said he didn't remember ever seeing a semicolon anywhere in his whole life; maybe they didn't have those when he was in school as a child. Mrs. Berry laughed and assured him that semicolons had been around a long time.

She told the class that the newspaper editor was there and said we probably use a lot of semicolons in the paper. I replied that I "almost never" use them. The teacher looked over a weekly newspaper written especially for beginning readers. No semicolons there.

The discussion had extended beyond the time for class to be over, so Mrs. Berry brought it to an end. But I'll bet those six students were on the lookout for semicolons the rest of the week.

By the way, I came back to the office and searched our Tuesday front page for semicolons. None of the four staff-written stories contained semicolons, but I found seven in two articles from the Associated Press. Of the seven, just one was used to join two sentences (or independent clauses); the others were used to separate items in a series.

But that's another lesson for another teachable moment.

Reprinted by permission of the author and the *Abilene Reporter-News*.

This piece is adapted from a speech by Elmer Kelton to the Texas Folklore Society in 1988. The full text of the speech is included in the book *Elmer Kelton Country: The Short Fiction of a Texas Novelist*. Kelton, who died in 2009, was voted by his fellow western authors as the greatest western writer of all time.

# Fiction Writers Are Liars and Thieves

Elmer Kelton

Someone has said that fiction by definition is a lie. By extension this means that fiction writers are liars. In that context I will admit to it, and go a step further. I will say that fiction writers are liars and thieves.

We steal stories wherever we find them, disguise them, paint them up like car thieves in a chop shop, then present them as our own. We watch people and steal their characteristics, give them to our fictional characters and call ourselves creative.

The beauty of it is that it is not against the law. Readers seem to see no harm in it. They'll even pay us well for doing it.

Dr. C. L. Sonnichsen once said that if you steal from one source you are a plagiarist. If you steal from ten sources you are a researcher. If you steal from fifty sources you are a scholar. My crime is greater than that.

For instance, in *The Time It Never Rained,* Charlie Flagg is the middle-aged rancher who serves as the main character. He struggles through the long seven-year drought of the 1950s, gradually losing a little here, a little there until he has lost most of what he owns, except for his dignity and his self-respect.

Many people have asked me if I modeled Charlie after their fathers. My mother believed he was modeled after *my* father. They are *all* right. I used so many things from so many people that Charlie Flagg is a little of all of them, but in total he is none of them.

Page Mauldin is another major character in the story, Charlie's best friend. Charlie is a small rancher, owning a little land, leasing some more. He is as big as he wants to be, nowhere near rich, but comfortable. Mauldin, however, is driven by ambition to be the biggest rancher in West Texas, and he just about is. But he is leveraged to the hilt and has his operations scattered all over the country. His size and his debts make him a lot more vulnerable even than Charlie, and eventually he loses everything.

To a very substantial degree, I modeled Page Mauldin after a real person, one of the biggest ranch operators in

West Texas in the 1940s and well into the 1950s. I knew him fairly well. Eventually, like Mauldin, he lost almost everything he had.

When the book came out, I was a little nervous that he would recognize himself in the story. I didn't see how he could possibly miss the connection if he read it. One day I ran into him at the San Angelo auction. He said, "I just read your book." I thought, "Oh God, here it comes."

He said, "You know, I sure did enjoy it. That old Charlie Flagg was just like me."

Fiction writers share one advantage with painters: if they don't like something where it is, they can move it.

In my mind, I set *The Time It Never Rained* in the area around Eldorado, south of San Angelo. It had many of the kinds of settings I needed, a good combination of ranchlands and farmlands. Now Eldorado is a nice town, but it doesn't have all the features I needed for my story. As an example, the book opens in the courthouse, and I wanted a nice Victorian courthouse, not a plain square type like Eldorado's. So I just moved the 1880s courthouse from Paint Rock down to Eldorado, which I called Rio Seco in the story.

We fiction writers often borrow from real historic personages, though we may not call them by their true names, and we weave a certain amount of fiction around them.

For instance, in *Stand Proud* you'll find a good bit of Charles Goodnight, under the guise of Frank Claymore. I am not the only one who has borrowed liberally from Goodnight. Ben Capps did it with his *Sam Chance.* Larry McMurtry did it in *Lonesome Dove.* I guess a lot of us owe some royalties to the Goodnight estate.

*The Day the Cowboys Quit* was loosely based on the cowboy strike at Tascosa in 1883. In real life, the cowboys lost the strike. Many of them stayed around, taking up land, running cattle of their own. The big ranchers regarded some of them as thieves. They hired Pat Garrett to ride around the country, be seen, and perhaps scare some of the undesirables into leaving. Garrett was by that time famous for having killed Billy the Kid.

I had a character roughly based on Garrett, but I could not bring him to full life. He seemed just a flat, two-dimensional villain. The story had a hole in it where that character was concerned.

One day I interviewed an elderly ranchwoman named Rachel Bingham at Spur, and she told me a story about an old-time gunfighter named Pink Higgins.

The ranchers there had been suffering some rustler problems and hired Pink Higgins to stop it. One day he met one of the main suspects, a cowboy, on horseback in the middle of the road. They both drew six-shooters, and the cowboy came out second. He was buried where he fell.

A headboard was put up to mark the grave, but cattle kept rubbing against it and knocking it over. Rachel's husband, Al Bingham, decided finally to put a little fence around the grave and protect it from the cattle. He put some posts and wire and lumber in his wagon and started off.

As he worked on the fence, who should ride up but Pink Higgins. Higgins asked him what he was doing. Bingham couldn't lie to him. He told him he was putting a fence around that grave to protect it. He waited nervously then, wondering what Higgins's reaction would be.

Higgins thought about it a minute, then said, "That's a good idea. I'll help you." He helped Bingham put a fence around the grave of the man he himself had killed.

I interpolated that into my story. Suddenly the gunfighter, called Lafey Dodge in the book, came alive as a real human being with more than one side to his character. I think that one scene helped make the book. And I owe it to Mrs. Bingham's story.

Several years ago John Graves said you should never tell a fiction writer a story you want to use yourself, because he will preempt it, give it a few twists and make it his own. I have always tried to be honest in most ways, but when it comes to good stories, I am as shameless a thief as you'll meet.

From *Elmer Kelton: The Short Nonfiction of a Texas Novelist* by Elmer Kelton, reprinted by permission of TCU Press.

# About the Editor

Glenn Dromgoole is the author of thirty books. A native Texan, he has lived in West Texas for more than thirty years. He is a former editor of the *Abilene Reporter-News*, and he and his wife, Carol, own Texas Star Trading Company, a Texas book, gift, and gourmet shop in downtown Abilene. He is cofounder and longtime chairman of the West Texas Book Festival in Abilene and was named Abilene's Outstanding Citizen of the Year in 2013.

An anthology of more than 30 heart-warming and humorous Christmas stories—all set in West Texas or by West Texas writers

# West Texas Christmas Stories

ISBN 978-0-89112-333-0 | 160 pages

EDITED BY GLENN DROMGOOLE

Christmas is a time for laughter and joy. Christmas is about faith and family and friendship, about Jesus and also Santa Claus, about giving and receiving. And Christmas is about storytelling.

Abilene Christian University Press

www.acupressbooks.com | 1-877-816-4455 toll free

STORIES FROM A SMALL TOWN
*with a Generous Scoop of Good Will*

# Coleman Springs USA

ISBN 978-0-89112-319-4 | 144 pages

GLENN DROMGOOLE

"Coleman Springs is a small town with a huge heart—full of interesting characters who will make you look forward to your next visit. Only problem is you won't want to leave."

—**Ben Rehder,** author of *Buck Fever*

# TEXAS STORIES
## I Like to Tell My Friends

**Real-life Tales of Love, Betrayal, and Dreams from the History of the Lone Star State**

T. LINDSAY BAKER

You will see Texas through the eyes of people who lived in the wild West you only read about in history books. Their fears, frustrations, and humor come alive in these amazing tales.

ISBN 978-0-89112-268-5 | 224 pages

Abilene Christian University Press

www.acupressbooks.com | 1-877-816-4455 toll free

# MORE TEXAS STORIES
## I Like to Tell My Friends

**The Tales of Adventure and Intrigue Continue from the History of the Lone Star State**

T. LINDSAY BAKER

From dreamers and schemers to would-be saints. They're all still out there on the cultural horizon, and Dr. Baker knows how to tell their tales with accuracy, respect, and a strong sense of place."

-**Dan K. Utley,** Chief Historian, ret.
Texas Historical Commission

ISBN 978-0-89112-354-5 | 192 pages